Praise fo

In a period in which the curriculum – ~~and even the~~ subject to ceaseless challenge and accountability, this welcome book overtly opens up the debate. Martin Robinson paints a picture of an education system in thrall to the Machine: a data-obsessed, narrowly instrumentalist, capitalist version of education, wherein metrics are cherished more than wisdom. However, passionate as he is for a liberal, dialogic curriculum, Robinson does not simply wish us to agree, or to succumb to his view, but rather to critically *engage*. And Robinson's assertions have relevance beyond schooling, given the recent onslaught of instrumentalist applications to higher education too. Whether you agree with his arguments or not, you will not fail to be stimulated by *Curriculum*.

Professor Becky Francis, Director, UCL Institute of Education

In this learned and accessible book, Martin Robinson explores the tensions at the heart of curriculum thinking – pointing to wisdom and the structures and systems likely to hinder it. Robinson tackles the reductionist, misconceived view of a knowledge-rich curriculum as a series of lists and urges us to regard it as a way of making meaning, of asking serious questions about how we live, of thinking about the values, ideas and objects that help to shape our lives and the larger landscape of human endeavour.

An important read for all school leaders.

Mary Myatt, author of *High Challenge, Low Threat*
and *The Curriculum: Gallimaufry to Coherence*

This is a very important book. While the dumb and brutal ugliness of instrumentalist education is all too familiar to many of us, never before has it been so clearly expressed or so convincingly unpicked and exposed. Martin Robinson's *Curriculum*, however, is much more than a depressing, defeatist explanation of why things have got as bad as they are. Instead it is a beautifully written love letter to the very substance of education, a triumphant and confident call to arms, and is ultimately the manifesto on which the fightback against the Machine should be based.

Ben Newmark, Vice Principal, Nuneaton Academy

Martin Robinson's *Curriculum* is an impassioned call to arms for educators to throw off the shackles of the Machine with its data-driven approaches and embrace a more human vision of education which puts the curriculum at its core. An astounding book on many levels which is destined to become the seminal work on what should be taught in our schools.

Dr Carl Hendrick, author of *What Does This Look Like in the Classroom?*

As the focus of our schools and academies turns to curriculum, in writing this book Martin Robinson has given us a timely paean to the polymath. Arguing that schools need to move beyond education as mundane transaction, Robinson imagines a broad and balanced curriculum designed to inspire and nourish wisdom.

Readable and uplifting in a way that many other contemporary education books are not, Robinson's achievement is to take the recognisable and commonplace in our schooling system and reframe it in such a way as to place it on a higher plane, while at the same time retaining its familiarity.

Robinson is the grizzled, eccentric and entertaining teacher in the corner of the country's staffroom: challenging assumptions, refusing to toe the line and with no time for the bright young things and their data-laden tablets. His is a much-needed voice of dissent in an era of mechanistic education.

Duncan Partridge, International Programme Development, Voice 21, and former director of education, The English-Speaking Union

Appealing both to teachers nervous of a return to Gradgrind's 'facts alone' and those troubled by the romantic ideals of progressivism, Robinson's *Curriculum* lays out with crystal clarity the questions confronting schools and their leaders in the aftermath of the turn away from a skills agenda and back to knowledge. Like a Virgil in tweed, he leads us on a fascinating journey down the corridors of our corporate-grey schools amid their perils of spreadsheets, tick-boxes, technology and bureaucracy – and shows that unless teaching and learning are understood as quests for human freedom, curriculum risks becoming yet another buzzword fad.

In a work infused with the same remarkable breadth of reading and grasp of detail that made *Trivium 21c* such an accessible but intellectually rich work, Robinson deftly sets out what school leaders, teachers, pupils and their parents must do if we are to discover the knowledge that will make us all wise.

Gareth Sturdy, teacher, journalist and co-author of *What Should Schools Teach?*

Curriculum is a timely, refreshing and enlightening follow-up to *Trivium 21c*. At a time when thousands of schools across the UK are wrestling with the challenge of curriculum design, all too often with a vision limited by the pressure to maximise outcomes, Martin Robinson leads us to the philosophical high ground – and it's a mighty relief.

The central metaphor of Athena versus the Machine captures the state of things perfectly, serving both as a warning and a call to arms. Tackling a broad range of issues – including whether knowledge can or should be 'powerful', the concept of cultural mobility, and the role of formal education in the context of educating for freedom – Martin reminds us continually that, far from the utilitarianism of the machine, education is deeply human and that knowledge 'helps us to understand who we are'. Martin challenges us to raise our sights, to think more deeply and expansively about the purpose of the curricula we provide and to remember who it's all for.

Intellectually, *Curriculum* towers above the field of functional books about schooling; a must-read for anyone looking to put some heart and soul into their curriculum.

Tom Sherrington, education consultant and author of
The Learning Rainforest and *Rosenshine's Principles in Action*

In his latest book, Martin adds to his earlier work on the Trivium and discusses the difference between a curriculum which serves 'Machine schools' and one which serves 'Athena schools'. His theory is that while it is essential to provide a knowledge-rich curriculum, it is the quality of the knowledge that matters. He goes on to ask difficult questions about who decides what a non-white, non-middle-class curriculum looks like, and makes the point that liberal arts are not set in stone and that tradition is ever-changing.

At a time when Ofsted (themselves a cog in Robinson's Machine analogy) has reignited the curriculum debate, *Curriculum* is a most timely publication and a thought-provoking read for anyone involved in our current school system.

Naureen Khalid, trustee of Connect Schools Academy Trust and
governor on the local governing body of Newstead Wood School

In *Curriculum*, Robinson explores what contemporary educational debate has sorely needed: a way to give real meaning and purpose to education beyond its mere capacity to generate wealth or power.

Michael Merrick, teacher, writer and speaker

In *Curriculum*, Martin Robinson tackles the central educational issue of our time: the contest between Athena (the goddess of wisdom) and the Machine (mechanical thinking and the quantification of learning). He reminds us, however, that the beating heart of the school lies in its curriculum, and assures us that there is still hope for 'bringing the human back' into education.

Written with Martin's customary elegance, wit and intelligence, *Curriculum* is an inspirational contemporary hymn to the teacher, warning us off settling for the click of the Machine when Athena beckons us to rediscover an education that gives meaning to life. It's destined to be one of the must-read books in the field.

Paul W. Bennett, Director, Schoolhouse Institute, Founding Chair, researchED Canada, and author of ten books on Canadian history and education

Written with meaning and human purpose – and with erudition, compassion and a real understanding of ground-level pressures facing the school machinery – this is the best book on curriculum that I have read. And at a time when curriculum as a concept and reality are up in the air across the UK, and moving in divergent directions, this is the text that brings us together in terms of what's really important in education, and what binds us. It needs to be read by everyone with a stake in our future.

Rajvi Glasbrook Griffiths, Deputy Head Teacher, High Cross School, Director, Literature Caerleon, and writer for *The Western Mail*, *Planet* and *Wales Arts Review*

Curriculum is a wonderfully inspiring, optimistic and deeply philosophical book that refocuses the purpose of education. Martin's style of writing and philosophical considerations are fascinating in provoking our thinking about the value of education and the reasons why we, as educators, come to work every day.

A must-read for educators, yes, but also for anyone who values the centrality of education in the pursuit of wisdom and the betterment of humanity.

Sam Gorse, Head Teacher, Turton School

Curriculum
ATHENA VERSUS THE **MACHINE**

MARTIN ROBINSON

Crown House Publishing Limited
www.crownhouse.co.uk

First published by
Crown House Publishing
Crown Buildings, Bancyfelin, Carmarthen, Wales, SA33 5ND, UK
www.crownhouse.co.uk

and

Crown House Publishing Company LLC
PO Box 2223, Williston, VT 05495, USA
www.crownhousepublishing.com

British Library of Cataloguing-in-Publication Data
A catalogue entry for this book is available from the British Library.

Edited by Peter Young

Print ISBN 978-178583302-1
Mobi ISBN 978-178583447-9
ePub ISBN 978-178583448-6
ePDF ISBN 978-178583449-3

Printed and bound in the UK by Charlesworth Press, Wakefield, West Yorkshire

To Olive, Kerry and Lotte, with love.

Contents

Acknowledgements

I must thank the following people who have helped this book see the light of day:

David Bowman for his patience and kindness; Peter Young and Emma Tuck for seeing the book through its gestation with wise counsel and great care; Beverley Randell for thoughtfully and diligently keeping me on my toes; Rosalie Williams, Tabitha Palmer and Daniel Bowen for their encouragement and ideas; Tom Fitton for his wonderful cover design; and, indeed, everyone at Crown House for sticking with this project throughout.

Thank you also to Tom Sherrington, Sam Gorse and Gareth Sturdy, and my mum, for their comments on the first draft, which helped me sharpen my focus and understand the whole book from fresh and different perspectives.

Finally, and importantly, my family and friends, who have helped more than they can know over a challenging couple of years, thank you.

Yes, 'twas Minerva's self; but ah! how changed,
Since o'er the Darman field in arms she ranged!
Not such as erst, by her divine command,
Her form appeared from Phidias' plastic hand:
Gone were the terrors of her awful brow,
Her idle aegis bore no Gorgon now;
Her helm was dinted, and the broken lance
Seem'd weak and shaftless e'en to mortal glance;
The olive branch, which still she deign'd to clasp,
Shrunk from her touch and wither'd in her grasp;
And, ah! though still the brightest of the sky,
Celestial tears bedimm'd her large blue eye:
Round the rent casque her owlet circled slow,
And mourn'd his mistress with a shriek of woe!

Lord Byron, 'The Curse of Minerva' (1812)

Introduction:

The Athena School

A god in the sense I'm using the word is the name of a great narrative, one that has sufficient credibility, complexity and symbolic power so that it is possible to organise one's life and one's learning around it. Without such a transcendent narrative, life has no meaning; without meaning, learning has no purpose.

Neil Postman, The End of Education (1996)

The 'great narrative' of too many of our schools is mundane, with the merely measurable as the pinnacle of meaning. Counting them in, counting them out; these schools employ mechanical metaphors. Each child is set on a 'flight path', and data and targets are worshipped rather than the symbolic, spiritual power of a god. Perhaps this is inevitable in a secular world, but is it wise? These schools bypass the quality of knowing something and replace it with destination data – knowledge is a means to an end rather than an end in itself. The focus is on the grade and not on the knowing.

Knowing is essential, it is the stuff of education, but what to know, why to know it and how to know it are not only essential questions, they are also impossible to answer fully with any degree of certainty. Yet there are those who search for objective answers to these questions by allying education to the instrumentalism that is extant in large numbers of schools.

Some of these instrumentalist aims take the form of justifying certain content by suggesting that it is essential for social mobility and/or social justice. Others insist on a pragmatic approach that *might* provide a march up the school exam league tables. And others see success in counting the number of pupils who leave the school to enter a 'top' university. In many schools, pupils have gone from being potential citizens to customers of an educational product, and now find themselves reduced to data points with a need to perform beyond expectations for their 'type'. Is this a meaningful pursuit? Whichever method is used to justify the content of a curriculum, can utilitarian/utopian aims (or their proxies) justify 13 years or so of full-time education?

This book argues for the study of knowledge for its own sake, but also that knowledge, alone, is not enough. Schools need to set up their pupils for the individual and communal pursuit of wisdom. This pursuit is animated by a god, Athena, while the overtly instrumentalist approach is represented by the Machine. While it is essential to provide a knowledge-rich curriculum, it is the quality of the knowledge that matters, and therefore it is within this subjective realm – where individual taste and thought is understood and nurtured, and the way we make meaning in the world matters – that the arguments in this book will be made. The qualitative approach will be set in direct opposition to the purely quantitative.

How does Athena help to provide us with the wherewithal to deliver a curriculum centred around the pursuit of wisdom?

Athena

Hephaestus wielded a giant axe and in one swift swing cut Zeus' head clean in two. Then, as Stephen Fry explains in *Mythos* (2018: 84–85), out stepped a female: 'Equipped with plated armour, shield, spear and plumed helmet, she gazed at her father with eyes of a matchless and wonderful grey. A grey that seemed to radiate one quality above all others – infinite wisdom.' Zeus' head repairs itself, and all who witness the birth of Athena realise that she has power beyond all other immortals.

Nietzsche (1969 [1883–1891]) pronounced that 'God is dead' and foresaw our struggles to create meaning. Without meaning, the school – the very place in which we should aspire to learn about the greatest thoughts and ideas – becomes the place where purpose is reduced to a list of target grades and performance measures that offer little in the way of true inspiration: the transcendent.

Athena has inspired many people across continents and civilisations, and now, most importantly, she can inspire us. Instead of asking what do the exam boards want, what does government want, what does the customer want, what does the market want, what do inspectors want, what does the data demand, we can aim higher: what does Athena want? What can Athena bring to our schools?

Athena is the goddess of philosophy, courage and inspiration. She is concerned with promoting civilisation and encourages strength and prowess. She brings order but can also rustle up a storm. She is the goddess of mathematics, strategy, the arts, crafts, knowledge and skills. She is the goddess of agriculture, purity, learning, justice, intelligence, humility, consciousness, cosmic knowledge, creativity, education, enlightenment, eloquence, power, industry and inventions – scientific, industrial and artistic. She is the patron of potters, metalworkers, horsemanship, women's work, health, music, navigation and shipbuilding. She is virginal but imbued with maternal cunning. She possesses magical powers. She is the protector of the state and social institutions. She is a teacher of many things, including working with wool. She is the goddess of law and just warfare. She is not afraid of a fight (she flayed the skin of Pallas and used it to make a shield) and can inspire others into battle. But she is able to put down her weapons when necessary because she is not driven by war. Athena is the goddess of wisdom.

Looking around at what some of our schools have become, we can see that wisdom has been sidelined. When the importance of knowledge is reduced by becoming part of an input–output model of measurable 'success', there is a need to move from the mechanistic systems that have caused this decline in value and to bring the human back in. Our attitudes and perspectives towards knowledge matter. The meaning we give to it matters – and the meaning it gives to us. If we think of curriculum as narrative, and realise that our stories are understood in many different ways, we begin to understand that being knowledge-rich is also about the many ways that knowledge is understood. These understandings are tied into value systems and the ways in which each of us makes meaning and that meaning is revealed to us. Curriculum, at its heart, can challenge us to reassess our values and understand meanings anew.

A curriculum that serves Athena is a very different beast to one that serves the Machine. An Athena approach to curriculum is an education that unashamedly pursues wisdom and extols the virtues of why to study. It asks, 'Children, do you want to be mind-full or mind-less? A free person or a slave?' Some might choose mindlessness – the easy, cynical way – but if we are to make a real difference to human lives then we should be offering more. Education can help to free us, and this freedom is first and foremost a freedom of thought.

The Greek creation myth involves Prometheus making human beings by shaping them from small lumps of clay. Athena breathed life into these figures – giving them their potential for wisdom and feeding their souls. A mechanical education works against freedom of thought, while Athena positively nurtures it. This is the joy of a liberal education.

A liberal education is shaped by its pursuit of wisdom, whereby the teaching and learning of knowledge are joined by the nurturing of experience and judgement. For the philosopher Michael Oakeshott (1989 [1975]: 22), 'Liberal learning is learning to respond to the invitations of the great intellectual adventures in which human beings have come to display their various understandings of the world and themselves.' It is, above all, an invitation to join in with the conversations that began at the beginning of time and that will continue long after our individual lives have ended. This is where the pursuit of individual wisdom interacts with and becomes enlivened by our communal, continual pursuit of wisdom.

If we decide to make this pursuit our central mission, how would it change our schools?

Part I

The Machine

Chapter 1

The Knowledge-Rich Curriculum

'We all teach knowledge' is one of the phrases used to argue against knowledge-rich approaches. It is easy to see how a problem might arise – indeed, we do all teach knowledge.

In many people's pockets and on many people's desks, a knowledge-rich environment is but a tap or a click away. There is a lot of knowledge out there on the internet and in the library; there is more easily accessible knowledge than anyone could learn in a lifetime. Knowledge is everywhere.

If by knowledge-rich we mean 'a lot of knowledge', it can easily be argued that each child could google to their heart's (and mind's) content every day, make changes to their long-term memories and tick the knowledge-rich box. But this would be facetious. A disorganised romp through 'facts' of varying degrees of veracity thrown up by a search engine is not a curriculum.

What makes knowledge rich is how it is organised. Knowledge is organised into subjects and disciplines which have their own ways of interrogating the world. It is organised by values – how we feel about the world and what is important to us. It is organised by narratives within and across subjects and disciplines which can open up arguments, clashes and disagreements on which people often pitch their identities. Knowledge is the stuff we marshal to help us find a place in this world; hence why the potential answers to 'what knowledge?' are so keenly felt.

Which is why knowledge on its own is not enough. Curriculum is the organisation of knowledge. It should help children to understand different ways of making meaning and how values enable us to respond to the world. Knowledge-rich is not rich at all if it fails to demonstrate the importance of the great controversies that allow human beings to argue about how we live and how we might live.

Educational approaches that use (so-called) purely objective data to justify the type of education a child receives falter because the very ground on which they stand tends not towards wisdom but the easily measurable. Whether these quantifiable measures are test scores, destination outcomes, average wage achieved or IQ, they will struggle to explain why a young person should study *Antigone* rather than *We Will Rock You*, other than implying that *Antigone* is somehow more 'acceptable' because we might find it referred to in a broadsheet newspaper. But *We Will Rock You* might be found there too, so this doesn't get us very far.

Some of the more astute among you might be shouting, 'We should study the things that engage our kids and are meaningful to their lives,' and that might be true, but what these things might be is not immediately apparent to any of us. What is 'meaningful' and, thereby 'truly engaging' to a life is not revealed instantly. It can take a lifetime of searching to find out that something we thought we knew can speak to us in an entirely new and enlightening way.

What we understand by 'knowledge-rich' and 'broad and balanced' in order to justify what we include – and what we leave out – matters. It matters because this is what helps to engage young people in making meaning in their lives, and this cannot be achieved with shallow, instantly gratifying, isolated chunks of information.

Whose knowledge, what knowledge and why are important issues, not just for theoretical debate, but as urgent questions that demand answers. Arguably, it was Matthew Arnold who set us on this course: he regarded certain knowledge as 'sweetness and light', as opposed to philistinism or barbarism (Arnold, 2009 [1869]). Whether the argument is 'knowledge is power' or 'knowledge is powerful', each agenda tries to justify itself in ways beyond the idea of what knowledge is best to know on its own terms. That those who have been educated about the finest things sometimes commit the grossest acts shows us that not all is sweetness and light in the knowledge stakes.

But if Arnold's approach is mistaken, is the only alternative on offer the philistinism of the marketplace, whether measured by exam scores or five stars on Amazon or Goodreads? A TripAdvisor approach might work for choosing a hotel for a two-week vacation in sunny Spain, but can we rely on popular choices to discern beauty and truth beyond what is immediately accessible? If we devalue the role of the curator and the connoisseur – and leave curriculum in the hands of populists, the market, exam scores and arguments around accessibility – then teachers really have given up.

What does this mean in practice? It means, without a doubt, that the curriculum should include *Antigone* and not *We Will Rock You*. This decision is shaped by our values, and Athena can help us realise what those values are. It is the quality inherent in what-is-to-be-learned that answers our questions about what to include. And yet, quite rightly, it also opens us up to many arguments. Prejudice, authority, tradition and intuition are very difficult to muster if they are the only ammunition you have on your side. This is again why knowledge alone is not enough. Making a list of things to be learned is a dispiriting task; many a reductive approach to curriculum design starts and ends with these lists. If we can glimpse something beyond the list – the cultural assumptions, arguments and structures of our storytelling – we can begin to understand what a good curriculum might be. This book argues that culture is an essential way that humankind makes sense of and engages with the world, and it is our duty to our young people to help them in this sense-making and engagement.

It might be that teachers can't explore these issues because they are trapped within mechanistic approaches. They might be preoccupied with data and test scores, obsessed with quantitative rather than qualitative measures. They might pay lip-service to quality but find themselves teaching in schools obsessed by systems. These schools, although often called 'factory schools', are more akin to 'office schools' and define themselves through varying degrees of accuracy and efficacy ('look at our score').

Athena cannot necessarily make children wise, but she can set them on the pursuit of wisdom and help them to develop their minds in tandem with the wisdom(s) of the time. Whatever we inherit genetically, it is what we come across culturally and socially that helps us to understand what we are and what we might be.

The mind is not an empty vessel awaiting knowledge: children come to school already equipped with stories and ways of making sense of the world. Curriculum can only make inroads into pupils' minds if we accept that some of what we teach is highly contested – challengeable as well as challenging. It is only by getting involved in these contestations that we can set our pupils' minds on the path towards wisdom. And we shouldn't just focus on the individual. Instead, we should also look at the community of minds as a whole and pursue wisdom as a collegiate affair.

The pursuit of wisdom is one we hold in common. It is a contract between the living, the dead and the unborn. It is either enhanced or degraded in our culture, institutions, schools and classrooms. Curriculum is not asking how well one child is performing, but how wise our studies are. If our pupils as a whole strike us as culturally impoverished, we have to ensure that our school culture enriches, broadly and deeply. We have to attend to our curriculum: is it rich enough? Is what we teach good enough?

However, the Machine is just a click away. It systematises, rather than humanises, by treating the human being as a measurable memory machine: pupils are reduced to 'programmes on computers made of meat' (Midgley, 1994: 9). They are components of an input–output system which focuses only on the extremely important aspect of memorisation, at the cost of the rather more qualitative 'why' or 'what is important'– on feelings, taste, discrimination, argument, thought, educated opinion and being able to express ourselves. If we simply view learning as being 'brain based', a mechanistic metaphor that leaves out the human being, then our education system will leave young people struggling to make meaning of their lives.

This book is partly a hymn to the teacher; instead of being seen as erstwhile office workers, with 'teaching' entailing delivering on the bottom line, Athena wants to re-energise the teacher as a member of the community of minds from which they emerged and into which they can introduce their progeny. This is why we went into teaching. This is our necessary mission.

But this is not possible if the teacher is caged inside the Machine.

The Iron Cage

Human nature is not a machine to be built after a model, and set to do exactly the work prescribed for it, but a tree, which requires to grow and develop itself on all sides, according to the inward forces which make it a living thing.

John Stuart Mill, *On Liberty* (1859)

In their 'Teacher Well-Being and Workload Survey: Interim Findings' (Scott and Vidakovic, 2018), Ofsted found that:

- 28% of respondents report low well-being at work, 26% medium, 35% high and 11% report very high well-being at work.

- 31% of teachers report low well-being at work compared with 18% for senior leaders.

- 25% of all respondents have been absent from work due to health problems caused or made worse by work, excluding accidents.

- 76% of teachers report that their job impacts negatively on their mental health and 60% report that it impacts negatively on their physical health.

- 62% of all respondents believe that teaching is not valued by society.

- The top three factors that positively affect respondents' well-being at work are children/pupils, colleagues and the support they receive from them.

- In contrast, the most frequently mentioned factors that negatively influence occupational well-being are behaviour (both pupils' challenging behaviour and inconsistent behaviour management by colleagues), workload and marking.

High workload and punishing marking regimes are prevalent in schools where a top-down management structure relies on numerous systems to deliver large amounts of data. When a school becomes overrun with people wielding (electronic) clipboards, spreadsheets outlining numerical targets for children and performance tasks for teachers, a culture of managerialism is holding sway. Even behaviour systems, rather than relying on teacher judgement, can become lost in a maze of criteria-based consequentialism. Managerialism imposes quantifiable administrative approaches as the correct way to run an institution, and in many ways it makes absolute sense. Efficiency is all, and though it is value-free in that what works tends to become more important than what is right, what else can be right other than what is rational?

The ideology of managerialism arose from business practices which have been repurposed for the non-profit school sector. But the business ethic doesn't fit easily into what should be an academy – a place where thinking is valued more highly than the bottom line. Managerialism comes at a cost to those who work and study in these institutions, and also to the qualitative experience of studying itself. The experience in the classroom should be one where the study of the subject, rather than the neediness of the bureaucracy, reigns supreme. The pursuit of wisdom should be paramount. Any interference with this ambition does a disservice to our great scholastic enterprise.

However, as employees become pawns in the game of delivery, the idea of management as neutral and post-ideological takes hold. The sociologist Max Weber referred to this as the 'iron cage' of rationality, where measurable goals shape the lives of people and institutions. Weber suggested that the iron cage was the inevitable result of Enlightenment thinking – that greater wisdom and freedom result from rationalisation. He wrote (quoting Goethe): 'For the "last man" (*letzten Menschen*) of this cultural development, it might well be truly said: "Specialist without spirit, sensualist without heart; this nullity imagines that it has attained a level of humanity (*Menschentums*) never before achieved" (Weber, 1992 [1904–1905]: 182). The ultra-rationalist approach of the efficient school deliberately attempts to remove the subjectivity of the teacher, regarding it as biased and problematic. And not without good reason: the teacher is a problem to be solved by way of scripted lessons, learning walks, lesson observations, marking criteria, planning checks, book checks, pupil voice, 'customer' surveys, lesson plan pro formas and elaborate discipline policies, all overseen by middle managers intent on micromanaging 'improvement'.

The alternative 'enchanted' world is a frightening place for those with a modern sensibility. It is full of magic and superstition, where God (or gods), fairies or spirits rule, and man has no dominion over nature but is part of it. Immediately we are faced with a ridiculous choice: if the options are 'rationality' or 'away with the fairies', then there really is only one answer.

But we need the mysterious world where subjective decisions are made. Flawed humans, with our conscious awareness of the world, need a space for our irrational desires, intuitive feelings and instinctive understandings of the *Lebenswelt* (life-world – our everyday experiences through which we make sense of the world and which occupy most of our time). By diminishing our range of judgement and making us question our own efficacy, systems replace human reasoning with (pseudo-)scientific precision.

Technology, bureaucracy, targets: they all ensure that we all become slaves to the Machine. The manager, with their flow charts and tick-boxes, is the lynchpin around whom all must be busy. Imposing a planned experience onto the workings of all can be damaging: 'In all its forms planning has a dangerous tendency to ignore the way in which, by the law of unintended consequences, the solution to one problem may be the start of another' (Scruton, 2010: 117).

Beware the heavily populated committees sending out edicts from on high, whether they are five-year plans for improvement or unwieldy initiatives with targets in tow. These are even more dangerous when 'supporting evidence' or 'reasons' are attached. If they claim that 'the science says …', 'the data shows …' or 'the aim is …', then the only way to listen is sceptically. The more complex the systems that schools have to operate, the more we will need an ever-growing army of leaders, managers and administrators to make sense of the consequences. This is the inevitable result of trying to run a school like a business or of treating education as a purely objective process, but is it wise?

The teachers who resist such changes are often derided: dissent might be the voice of the dispossessed (as well as, sometimes, the ignorant). Schools need opportunities for teachers to work together. And to enable tacit expertise to grow, they need fewer leaders planning, fewer edicts from above and more collective approaches that enable teachers to concentrate on the beating heart of the school – the curriculum. All teachers in a school should have a say in how the curriculum works, not through endless committee meetings but real power to design the curriculum, its delivery and assessment. Crucially, this power is not about individual teachers acting autonomously, but collegiate teams of subject specialists working together. Agreement among equals represents the checks and balances in the system, rather than serving the needs of an over-burdensome bureaucracy.

In the rational world, we aim to control nature, control systems, control classrooms, control knowledge, control kids – all of which can be overcome in the pursuit of the grade. Through Athena, our aim is to develop the emotional by giving young people the words through which they can articulate their experiences. The dance steps. The heart and voice with which to sing. But the mechanistic teacher is not expected to venture too far into the subjective world. They are required to teach texts that are accessible to the pupil/customer/data point in a way that alleviates rather than explores their suffering. Every poem has an explanation. Every artwork is a system of explicable symbols. Classrooms become sheltered spaces where unthreatening knowledge is rendered 'safe to know' because this is the easiest way to get the grades. Give them easy texts, short texts, texts that contain no upsetting moments, get through them at pace. When this is the ethos, we know something is wrong.

A culture of pure utility – where everything is systematised and measured, where all meaning is reduced to a number and where all conspire to accept this as the most important factor – is not the education we need for our children.

Welcome to the Machine

Many schools have become utilitarian business-minded ventures, all open-plan and specially designed streamlined systems. Machine-thinking technology, the machines in the Machine, has become ubiquitous. These office schools are managerialist, bureaucratic and imbued with business-like efficiency. The child as data point at the intersection of various categories (gender, class, ethnicity, age, performance pointers) is a sort of mini-machine – with all too human flaws that have the potential to skew the data analysis. So the system is designed to spot deviance: if a pupil makes a mistake, a call to action sets off an intervention.

These leadership-centred institutions set targets, check outcomes and are hot on efficient delivery. Teachers are micromanaged. Everything that can be measured will be measured. The language of leadership is about the effective delivery of stated objectives: what is your score on a scale of 1–9? Examination results are key. Curriculum is, paradoxically, an afterthought, almost incidental to the main business in hand, which is numbers. In wise schools, curriculum has always been the central concern, but in machine schools, teachers dispose of the baggage of caring about the meaning of what is studied, and why, and replace it with traffic-light, colour-coded spreadsheets where numerical targets are the order of the day. As long as they can deliver the bottom line, the quality of what teachers teach is of secondary interest.

The central concern of this brand of education is the efficiency of the various modes of fact transference. This encapsulates the vision of the Machine – successful transfer requires the conjuring of data points that are objective and quantifiable. In order for this to be done well, it is necessary to know the best way to get a piece of knowledge from one brain (the teacher's) into another brain (the pupil's). This knowledge must be retained. The process must be measurable and it must, quite rightly, be measured fairly. So the question arises: how can we find ways to create the most effective and efficient education system? In a competitive world, the Machine requires constant tinkering to ensure that it is running smoothly and better than other machines. Facts, evidence, measurement and 'what works' are rigorous necessities.

The professional teacher is immured in this all-encompassing vision. They – and, indeed, their pupils – are in the service of the efficient delivery Machine.

Chapter 2

Social Mobility

… all my means are sane, my motive and my object mad.

Herman Melville, *Moby-Dick* (1851)

The purpose of education is often couched in utilitarian or utopian language. The argument is made that a school's curriculum should provide pupils with the skills necessary for the 21st century job market and/or to ensure that they will grow into better people with the character required to create a better society.

When the Machine is made to service a meritocratic world in which all children are destined to rise up the ladder of social mobility, perversely, it seems to result in most children retaining the social status of their parents. (The prerequisite for some to fall off the ladder and regress from the status of their parents is not addressed.)

The all-pervasive idea of social mobility – the true meritocracy in which everyone can find the position they deserve and where educational performance is treated as a fair system of segregation – seems to make a lot of sense. The meritocratic ideal suggests you will do well at school if you are talented, and consequently you will do well at life and earn the wage that your talents deserve. But is this accurate?

The Meritocracy

The author of the great 1945 Labour Manifesto, Michael Young, came up with the term 'meritocracy'. He points out that 'If meritocrats believe … that their advancement comes from their own merits, they can feel they deserve whatever they can get. They can be insufferably smug … The newcomers can actually believe they have morality on their side' (Young, 2001). For Young, meritocracy is dystopian. He is right: the socially mobile utopian dream gives pupils the impression that the system is fair, so if they try hard – if they have a 'growth mindset' or adopt certain character traits that lead to success in life – they will succeed. Everyone can become prime minister, a pop star, a media mogul, an entrepreneurial billionaire or marry into royalty – just as long as they pass the required exams.

But the idea that those who do well in life do so entirely due to their own efforts is a pipe dream. We are not are born tabula rasa or with identical heritable genetic 'gifts' and cultural traditions. We do not live in identical environments and do not live identical lives in which we are all treated the same. A poor camel might find it easier to get into heaven than a rich human, but the latter will tend to keep the spoils in their own earthly paradise, secure behind electric gates. And, for some, cutting off one avenue to success will soon see another one opening up. It is not enough just to grumble that 'the system is unfair'. It is always possible for some individuals to beat the system, whether through luck, judgement, genetic gifts or the 'who you know' lottery. In addition, we have a global elite of lucky celebrity 'intellectualpreneurs' who believe their own hype, write books and deliver TED Talks, telling everybody else, 'If only you were more like me … just buy my self-help book/DVD.'

Hannah Arendt put it in the following way: 'Meritocracy contradicts the principle of equality … no less than any other oligarchy' (Arendt, 1954). For those who don't do well in school, in work and in life, the only consolation we can offer in a meritocracy is, 'Well, it's your own fault! You should have done better at school.' Education should be a consolation when people fall on hard times, not another hammer to hit them over the head with.

Despite our socially mobile aims, Alan Milburn, former chair of the UK's Social Mobility Commission, writes: 'The rungs on the social mobility ladder are growing further apart. It is becoming harder for this generation of struggling families to move up' (Social Mobility Commission, 2016: iv). It is not the fault of those involved in schooling that this is happening. It is down to economics, commerce and globalisation – factors over which education has little control. Yes, we can do our bit, but to ignore these outside pressures and declare that education is the one-stop shop for success in life is to put ridiculous and undue stress onto both teachers and children.

Education should do far more than produce fodder for the job market. Every CEO dripping in diamonds – and every down-and-out dripping in blood, sweat and tears – needs an education that offers them more than a first step to either triumph or tragedy. What seems to have passed us by is the fact that economic success tends to breed better education provision in a country, rather than a country performing better economically because of good education provision.

Utopia

The 'why' of schooling is often framed in a utopian way. The reason for education, it is suggested, is to create better people and a better world, so global education companies and national governments sell a vision of a bright future. Sometimes this is presented in ambiguous terms, sometimes in meritocratic terms and sometimes in both.

Pearson (UK) claims: 'Whether it's at home, in the classroom or in the workplace, learning is a never-ending road of discovery, challenge, inspiration, and wonder. At Pearson, we create tools that provide opportunities for learners at every stage of their journey. Because wherever learning flourishes, so do people.'[1]

---

1   See https://www.pearson.com/uk/.

The Department for Education in England states: 'We work to achieve a highly educated society in which opportunity is equal for children and young people, no matter what their background or family circumstances.'[2]

In the United States, education is linked explicitly to the economic performance of the country. The US Department of Education declares that their 'mission is to promote student achievement and preparation for global competitiveness by fostering educational excellence and ensuring equal access.'[3]

The educational aims of less liberal regimes are similarly idealistic. The seventeen responsibilities of the Ministry of Education in the People's Republic of China include the duty 'to direct the work of ideology and political education, moral, physical, health, arts, and national defence education in all types of schools at various levels; and to direct the construction of the Party in institutions of higher learning.'[4] In North Korea, every citizen has to learn the Ten Principles for the Establishment of the One-Ideology System. It is intrinsic to the management of schools and education ministries to have an all-encompassing vision that is communicable and measurable in some way.

In England, an organisation called PiXL, which is results and outcomes oriented, has branched out into 'character education' in which it offers a 'quick start' ' "off-the-shelf" character curriculum' that is designed to 'equip students with the skills, knowledge and competencies … that will help them succeed in the future.'[5]

Who could want for more than an off-the-shelf character? Education as a banal transaction in a DIY store? Now that we are outcome oriented, we have the promise of a delightful future: all children have potential, all are equipped with the right skills and character, all use the right technology and are managed by the right systems. But the future utopia is built on dodgy foundations.

---

2   See https://form.education.gov.uk/.

3   See https://www2.ed.gov/about/landing.jhtml.

4   See http://en.moe.gov.cn/About_the_Ministry/What_We_Do/201506/ t20150626_191288.html.

5   See https://www.pixl.org.uk/edge.

Utility

Utopian objectives are mixed with utilitarian aims and business-savvy outcomes. It is accepted almost without comment that education should mould young people into work-ready citizens, destined for a life of servitude in a global corporation. School is a journey for acquiring the skills needed to build the economy for the greater good.

The Machine must provide abundant opportunities for pupils to develop the three Cs (collaboration, creativity and critical thinking) for the workplaces of the future, because in these places everyone must be able to grasp new technology and produce copious amounts of stuff. However, young people will go on to work in systems where, paradoxically, creativity is frowned upon and collaboration means to conform to a call-centre-like script. No critical thinking here, thank you very much. The three Cs are bandied about as meaningless slogans more suited to a branded T-shirt than a way of life. The corporate three Cs are nothing like their authentic avant-garde counterparts, which harbour potentially dangerous possibilities rather than the safer ones beloved by the managerialists.

What is it like to be a pupil in this nirvana of exceptional achievement? Equipped with the STEM skills (science, technology, engineering and maths), perhaps with a bit of art thrown in for the 'skill' of empathy, are they ready for the workplace of the future where they may have to 'compete with artificial intelligence'?

When we get down to the nitty-gritty of visualising what this all looks like in the classroom, we often come unstuck. Meritocratic utopian utility and a big thinking vision might appear great when discussed in a professor's study, all efficient and streamlined. But when this comes into contact with humanity – pupils and teachers: brazen, debased, glorious, imperfect and individual – who don't share the vision, the system stutters. The longed for utopia can't contend with those who don't want to live in it. The contradiction is too great; individualisation is an inconvenience. This inconvenience is someone's daughter, son, mother, husband, brother, sister. Should we be demanding that they sacrifice their own needs in the service of the 'greater good'? If we only teach with an ideal future in mind, how do we deal with those who do not share our vision? Human experience can be a nuisance for the Machine.

Utility and utopia take us away from the day-to-day purpose of what is being studied in search of some far-off aim which detracts from the meaning of our studies in the present. Curriculum should not be seen as a series of hoops to jump through or hurdles to leap over on the way to somewhere else. Instead, it should be regarded as a way of making meaning, of asking serious questions about how we live, of thinking about the values, ideas and objects that help to shape our lives.

Chapter 3
The Single Vision

It makes sense to keep it simple when setting out a school vision. But if that simplicity ends up hampering different and complex ways of seeing the world, then we are not presenting a broad and balanced view and our curriculum is not knowledge-rich. If art is treated in the same way as science, then we lose the remarkable insights of both. Mechanistic approaches to schooling can do real harm to our different ways of interrogating the world.

The environment in which we live is shaped by algorithms and branding. Education is no different. Some of the UK's most famous independent schools have a global brand that is marketed in the international schools market. Even the local 'bog standard' school now, usually, has a website to sell itself to the market. Such brand awareness needs simple messages and a unified identity: 'we are a strict school', 'we are a restorative justice school', 'we are a knowledge school', 'we are a forest school'. In a system extolling choice, parents and pupils need to know what they are getting quickly. Although, strangely, for a good number of parents and children there is little or no choice at all: they get allocated a school place whether they like the brand or not.

The management team of a multi-academy trust also has a brand to protect and/or project. In an efficient trust, the mechanisms of the office school are dictated from a central hub which promotes quick responses. Teachers and pupils are shaped by the needs of the bureaucracy and teaching is delivered in line with the demands of the brand. They know how to do one thing and they need to do it successfully. The Machine must deliver. Schools have a single vision which is obeyed across the trust. The super-organisation, overseen by a CEO, regards order as the way forward, encompassed in a slogan and an institutional way of doing things. The vision is justified by the bottom line. And if the bottom line isn't met, then another multi-academy trust is ready to pounce with a corporate takeover and a different machine (or perhaps it's the same old machine with better branding?). All of them offer 'The Answer' to your school's woes, whether via technology, consultancy, products, lesson plans, textbooks, behaviour systems or 'what science says is the best way to teach'.

The brand is sometimes so narrow as to render any way of doing things differently, or even seeing things differently, completely off limits. When this unity of purpose becomes so destructive of alternative ways of seeing the world, and ourselves, then it is no longer sustainable to regard a school as a place for the pursuit of wisdom.

The problem with a single unifying vision is what to do with those individuals who don't fit in – the awkward squad who ruin it for everyone. If you are preparing children for a fantastic future full of eye-catching technology and artificial intelligence, what do you do about your stone masonry course, your Latin lessons or your ancient history syllabus?

What about the child who doesn't see a place for themselves in this marvellous world? How will your liberal outlook be perceived through the eyes of a young conservative, or your conservative outlook through the eyes of a young radical? And what would be the point of studying for this world if you have no future – if you have a debilitating illness and know you will die before you get old?

What about the subjects where assessment isn't all that accurate – those subjects that are much too subjective? How do you manage those teachers who don't believe that measuring progress every fortnight is possible? Or those pupils who don't give a f**k?

The Machine really doesn't like them.

Hedgehog or Fox?

In his essay, *The Hedgehog and the Fox*, Isaiah Berlin (1953: 22) writes: 'there exists a great chasm between those, on one side, who relate everything to a single vision … and, on the other, those who pursue many ends, often unrelated and even contradictory, connected, if at all, only in some de facto way.' For Berlin, foxes are those individuals who are drawn to infinite variety and hedgehogs are drawn to a coherent system which does one thing well.

A good school has an inbuilt fear of chaos and disorder, and rightly so. But does this mean that a successful school has to be highly centralised and controlling?

A human life story is complex – many unrelated elements are connected together in one person. What happens when we put all of these stories into an institution that is not only a collection of individuals, but also of many ways of seeing, interpreting and shaping the world? We have a school which defines itself thus: 'I am large, I contain multitudes' (as Walt Whitman put it about himself).

A school is large, it contains multitudes: subjects, teachers, pupils, parents, communities, nationalities, books, artefacts, histories, ways of thinking and all the other paraphernalia of a great education. In Berlin's parlance, a school curriculum must be more fox than hedgehog, and yet the management of schools – with their propensity to follow a centralising creed – tends to be more hedgehog than fox. This contradiction is at the heart of many of the problems in education.

Curriculum, by its nature, pursues many things in many different ways. But the machine school is a hedgehog – results and centralised systems all the way. Something has to give. Up until now, it has usually been curriculum.

Culture or Anarchy?

The Machine worries about the thrall of anarchy. The centralised system ensures that certain things are done in certain ways: registers, marking schemes, homework directives, uniform policies. There are rules about walking on the right side of corridors and up and down stairwells. There are rules about everyone standing when a visitor comes into the room. And the queue – oh, for order! In a world of rationality versus irrationality, there is only one way to go. The rational world is what we hope for ourselves because madness lies in the other. As teachers, we hanker after discipline and obedience, so we create ordered systems to serve this ideal. Mark this way! Test this way! Walk this way!

With incapable management the school is a work of chaos. Bullying, pushing and shoving is the order of the day. We find teachers either locked behind classroom doors or skulking in the staffroom, staring into the middle distance and longing to get out. Responsible parents do their best to avoid chaotic schools where many pupils live in fear. An anarchic school is a wilderness, a place of danger for pupils and staff. We must avoid chaos, so the thinking goes, therefore we must need efficient managerial systems.

But does our desire to create efficient systems crush much of what we ought to achieve?

Management

The Machine is leader obsessed. There are leaders throughout the system, promoted to manage the Machine, to create (and measure) new ways of doing things, to perfect the Machine. The problem with too many leaders is that they spoil the brand. Every leader is encouraged to initiate change, evaluate change and then, when they find out how little it actually achieves, quietly abandon said change (and don't tell anyone else in case they get labelled as incompetent).

Change is unceasing. Performance management targets ensure that schools are infected with initiative-itis: new innovations are introduced before the last one has even been evaluated. If we are spending more thinking time on initiatives than on teaching, then we have a problem.

The systems in which we all are engaged in the pursuit of utopian and utilitarian ideals seem to make sense. The Machine needs order and neatness: the demonstration of busyness beloved by bureaucrats (although the intelligent teacher is minded to throw a spanner into the works). The Machine is a slick data management system, turning on and off whenever and wherever required. Feedback drives feed-forward. If the data shows that a pupil's performance progress has slipped, the Machine flicks into action and all systems are go.

The feedback loop is never-ending. How well are we doing? How do we know? That feedback is an obsession should come as no surprise – the Machine is driven by it.

Where does curriculum thinking, more fox than hedgehog, fit in?

Chapter 4

The Singularity

The Machine as metaphor is being made real in our schools. Machine systems and machine learning are very real challenges for everyone involved in education. Schools use digital tools to communicate, to track and to collect data on pupils. In some education theories and practices, even pupils' minds are treated as if they are machines. Machine thinking makes an Athena approach to schooling all but impossible.

According to Google's director of engineering, Ray Kurzweil, 'By 2029, computers will have human-level intelligence … That leads to computers having human intelligence, our putting them inside our brains, connecting them to the cloud, expanding who we are' (Sulleyman, 2017). The businessman Elon Musk believes that to avoid irrelevance humans will have to merge with machines (Griffin, 2016). When a child is described as being lost in a book, it is a metaphor, an explanation of an emotional event. But the idea of digitalised humans forever lost in the Machine is in a different league altogether. And it is just around the corner: Musk believes that computer games will soon become 'indistinguishable from reality' and that virtual reality will become more than virtual – it will become our reality. And he uses this argument to suggest that we will soon be living in a virtual reality simulation.

Others might not go as far as Musk, but they do like the notion that we will become part of a 'hive mind'. In some corners of the tech-enthusiast world, the idea that our brains could be uploaded to the cloud is pervasive. Some even think that this technological advancement is inevitable, and that as a consequence many jobs will vanish or be altered irrevocably. For example, the advent of autonomous, driverless vehicles means that we can expect driving jobs to disappear in the next stage of (and I use the word advisedly) progress.

If the very nature of the self is under threat, then I am on the side of humankind. There is much to laud in new technologies, but I baulk when it comes to giving up too much of my humanity to the Machine. I don't mind a machine doing my washing; I do mind if a machine does my thinking. It is the futurologist's dream to have big changes just around the corner, but then changes have always been just around the corner. It is the trajectory of these changes that should concern us today.

For the contemporary teacher, what was a once a manageable job has become frantic – from passive-aggressive email pings demanding immediate action at any time of day or night to demands for a quick response to 'worrying' new data. These interruptions are intensifying our deeply felt anxiety about demonstrating that we are on top of things.

A swift reply to an email shows that we are in control, right? Wrong. The Machine has taken control. We are now writing reports, marking work, responding to pupils' and parents' demands at all hours. 'You haven't responded my email,' says a follow-up email sent two hours later. While trying to keep up, we are also chasing and collecting data, feeding the register and mark book into the Machine, but are still getting memos demanding, 'Why have you let this child fall behind?' The tools we use have started to use us.

Traditionally, we used the metaphor of things 'running like clockwork', with the tick-tock resembling a human heartbeat, but now everything works at a much faster pace. More data is needed and more data is churned out. In the highly reasonable aim of efficiency, teachers are left feeling bereft. Burnout is all too obviously, and inefficiently, human.

Teacher as Robot

The creatures outside looked from man to machine, and from machine to man, and from man to machine again; but already it was impossible to say which was which …

During a talk at the British Science Festival in 2017, the vice-chancellor of the University of Buckingham, Sir Anthony Seldon, suggested that machines would replace teachers within ten years:

> The machines will be extraordinarily inspirational.
>
> You'll still have the humans there walking around during school time, but in fact the inspiration in terms of intellectual excitement will come from the lighting-up of the brain which the machines will be superbly well-geared for.
>
> The machines will know what it is that most excites you and give you a natural level of challenge that is not too hard or too easy, but just right for you. (Sky News, 2017)

Here we have the redundancy of human agency writ large. The idea that we need constant excitement – the brain 'lighting-up', education as entertainment – is one thing, but the suggestion that the human is merely a servant to the Machine is another. Apparently, in the brave new world, teachers will be on hand merely to 'set up equipment, help children when necessary and maintain discipline' (Keay, 2017).

Replacing teachers with silicon chips won't take place overnight; instead it is happening piecemeal. Each step towards the deskilled teacher seems like the next logical stage, but look closely and it is clear that we are moving imperceptibly towards a system where the teacher is driven by the Machine. From emails to internet-sourced resources, to online video lessons, to interactive sessions, to guide-on-the-side enabling, to personalised learning, to scripted lessons, to online assessments, to project-based learning, to Silicon Valley conglomerate-sponsored teachers, to robot teachers … each step seems reasonable and 'modern'. Curriculum will not be a concern in the self-directed future.

In *The Rise of the Robots*, Martin Ford (2016: 73) writes that 'as work becomes ever more specialized it may … become more susceptible to automation'. Experience, knowledge and judgement become algorithmic processes in which wisdom itself is farmed out to the Machine. This is what is happening to teachers. Gradually, as speed and availability become the hallmark of what material is deemed suitable, teachers devalue their practice by downloading material from the internet. What is important is what is accessible from the interactive whiteboard. Is it fun? Will it engage the short attention spans of the Snapchat (or whatever is the latest app-chat) kids? Within all this engagement, the Machine even purports to show the teacher how their pupils are progressing and how good a teacher they are.

If human teachers are flawed and can't keep up with the demands of the Machine then, surely, it would be fairer to all concerned to replace them with artificially intelligent robots? A robot won't tire, it won't need a break and it won't go on strike, and although it might crash, it can be serviced by a small team of machine operatives. We would need to devise some laws of engagement about machine teaching but that could be done quite easily. The Machine would need to ensure that the robot teachers kept within certain parameters – we wouldn't want them to start teaching about computing and nothing else …

But can a non-human, no matter how advanced, educate a human being properly? For me, the answer is no. A machine cannot empathise or understand the human condition. It can only respond to certain inputs. It is by no means certain that a machine will ever even understand itself, let alone a human being. Cold-hearted rationalism has its place – it could have a useful role in instruction or training – but not in the fundamentally human-to-human relationships that are central to the common pursuit of an authentic education. Curriculum has to be delivered with a human face because it is a conversation that takes place between people who are aware of, and try to understand, each other.

Meanwhile, the system continues to demand efficiency and measurable progress. It requires this of pupils, of teachers, of management systems, of schools and of countries. Staying still is the new going backwards.

Cybernetics and the Thermostat

The American mathematician and philosopher Norbert Wiener defined cybernetics as the scientific study of control and communication in the animal and the machine. Nowadays, it is most often thought of in terms of the technological control and communication in systems. Cybernetic systems rely on causal loops: something is communicated which prompts a reaction, which is then adjusted in some way and sets up a feedback loop which determines what will be communicated next. In a machine, cybernetic thinking is centred around things that can be objectively measured.

The measures of success frequently used in schools are the exam grades the pupils achieve. If the grades slip, this alerts the management that action needs to be taken, but most institutions want to make sure that the slippage doesn't occur in the first place. In order to feed this continual need for success, progress is measured often and interventions are made when problems are found.

This method of communication and control is via feedback loops. There are positive feedback loops and negative feedback loops. A positive feedback loop amplifies an effect – for example, acoustic feedback occurs when sound from the speaker gets into the microphone and cycles around the system. A negative feedback loop causes a decrease in function: a good example is a thermostat which regulates temperature to keep it constant. If a room gets too warm, the thermostat feeds this information back to the boiler which then switches off; when things cool down it will switch back on again.

For this kind of regulation to work in a school, continual and accurate measurements need to be captured and communicated. Mechanistic systems monitor the child to find out whether they are progressing towards a predetermined target. If a child is not making sufficient progress, the Machine decrees instant intervention. Once the pupil has achieved the given target, the aim is to use regular monitoring to make sure they remain at that level.

However, there is often a paucity of objective measurement, despite persistent attempts to control the learning process and its often intangible output. If the system is built around a simple output (grade measures), then we might feel the effects of the law of unintended consequences. Quite simply, a child's progress in learning cannot be simply or continuously measured; we are not dealing with a thermostat. If deviation from a grade is treated as the only useful indicator of how a child is doing, then it must be accepted as an accurate measure. The problem is, of course, that a grade awarded by one teacher is not necessarily the same as that awarded by another. Grading a piece of work is not the same as sticking an electronic thermometer in a patient's ear. What is being measured does not give up its information that easily. The grade which apparently shows that a child is slipping behind might not be telling us what we think it is, and therefore there is little chance that the intervention deemed to be necessary will have a predictable result. The child is seen to drop a few marks, but instead of focusing on the learning, the focus becomes the grade. The system gets in the way of good, responsive teaching. A teacher is able to act quicker and more effectively in the classroom, responding to how a child is grappling with their learning, than a centralised system, responding to grades, ever can. Actual learning should never take second place to the grade.

Furthermore, there has never been a serious attempt at comparative grading, even with GCSE results. In externally marked exams, no one knows whether a 9 in physics is equivalent to a 9 in art. How could they? There is no way to ensure that our measures are commensurate. Even so, a grade slippage in English is seen as having the same significance as one in maths. Fall a point behind in an arts subject and the intervention is as instant as with a performance slip in calculus. But maths is far easier to grade accurately than the ephemeral subject of practical drama. If every subject was open to objective judgement, perhaps the system would work. But many arts subjects exist in the subjective realm, where feeling and gut instinct have to be our guides in a substantial amount of the work done. The only way to alleviate this is to destroy the very art that is being measured.

Even so, many teachers are expected to feed back 'accurate' assessments once every half term or so. While the teacher is tasked with trying to sum up a pupil's work in art in a single number, the pupil is faced with a set of grades which purport to tell them some sort of objective truth about their progress and whether they are on course for doing well in a future exam. That a pupil's performance can be reduced in such a way should concern us deeply, but the idea that the 'thermostat' approach reveals truths about a child's engagement with the subject matter that they are being taught should concern us more. There is no precise measure, no exact 'temperature' to take. In the pursuit of wisdom, tackling the subject matter in hand is far more important than trying to give this struggle a number. And if a number is stamped onto this struggle, it is likely that the child will believe the myth and think of themselves as a 4, 5 or 6, rather than as a potentially thoughtful person engaged in the lifelong pursuit of finding meaning.

The inimitable Rebecca Allen, former professor of education at University College London's Institute of Education and founder of FFT Education Datalab, has observed:

I'm no longer sure that *anybody* is creating reliable termly or annual pupil progress data by subject … Perhaps we don't really need to have accurate measures of pupil progress to carry on teaching in our classrooms. Education has survived for a long time without them. Perhaps SLT and Ofsted don't really mind if we aren't measuring pupil progress, so long as we all *pretend* we are. *Pretending* we are measuring pupil progress creates pressure on teachers through the accountability system. Perhaps that's all we want, even if the metrics are garbage. (Allen, 2018; original emphasis)

Repeatedly intervening with the intention of creating a climate in which a pupil will do better and better doesn't always work as intended. The pupil may become bamboozled by change and end up exhausted or resistant to further intervention, which might involve extra lessons, a teacher informing them about the virtues of a growth mindset or their parents/carers being called into school. In the worst case, the loop ends with the young person leaving the institution not knowing or understanding much of what they have been taught. It is a given that pupils' experience of the curriculum suffers. They are institutionalised via mechanical measurement systems and targets and by institutional language couched in terms of 'progress' or 'learning to learn' strategies which are generic and therefore divorced from curriculum content.

A curriculum can be made impenetrable by overzealous and nonsensical grading. We should focus our attention on helping children to think about the things that matter and to be invigorated by the content of the curriculum, not encourage them to stress about constant monitoring (expressed through grades and levels) or to become reliant on the interventions driving them through the system.

Various organisations have tried to create output systems which (they hope) will make a virtuous circle out of the feedback loop ideology. The result is a range of targets and goals which have transformed the system into one big feedback loop. 'Levels' were the most obvious example of this, and so are countless measurement tools that purport to determine skills, happiness and character traits.

In *Blueprint: How DNA Makes Us Who We Are*, the world's foremost behavioural geneticist, Robert Plomin, writes about how all this 'frenetic' teaching to chase league table positions for schools and exam scores for children makes very little difference to the overall performance of the school or the child. Instead, he suggests that we should focus on creating an environment in which children can enjoy learning. It is, after all, the 'qualitative nature of teaching' that matters (Plomin, 2018: 87).

The problem is an age-old one of causality versus correlation. Schools are in the business of equating success with the interventions they make. But as is always the case, correlation does not presuppose causal connection, however obvious the connection might seem. Valid intervention can only work where causality is proven. But proving such connections is the business of research, and research is much too time-consuming for busy schools, so they revert to relying on causal myths that suggest useful correlations. In order to keep progressing, they are always ready to take on board the next big thing. Causality is often ignored in order for the school to maintain the idea that the institution is the driver of success. The end result is that schools operate within a multiplicity of feedback loops – some of which might be working in opposition to others.

Given a chance, the human factor in any system will mess things up: every teacher will focus on their particular concerns and some of them will do well and others won't. The results may have little to do with their actions, but given the human capacity for generating stories that 'explain' what has happened, it may be easier to attribute causality to the Machine rather than to their own interventions. It is the old 'I was just following orders' gambit. It may be less stressful to find yourself as a slave to the Machine.

'What works' is a useful mantra; obviously, we don't want to do things that don't work in schools. But what works is usually established by measurement, which implies that any approach taken in a more subjective area is somehow lesser because it has not been shown to work within the parameters set by the particular measure chosen. This can be seen in schools which ensure a strict 'teaching to the test' approach: it might work in terms of results, but at what cost in terms of overall education?

Curriculum has had to live alongside instrumentalism for some time, and although I expect that measurement and efficiency will always have a place in schooling, it is evident that instrumental approaches can dismantle the focus on curriculum. Curriculum design is an art, not a science, and thus the judgement about what makes a curriculum work is mainly in the subjective realm. As such, schools that focus on target grades, measurable outcomes and 'mindset' approaches to achievement will ensure that mechanistic approaches win the day.

Curriculum is how we bring the human back in and sideline the Machine.

Human Life Distracted

Modern man can live, and should live … in his cities and in his machine shops with the same kind of swing and exuberance that the savage is supposed to have in his forest.

Ezra Pound, *Ezra Pound and Music* (1948)

The word 'savage', with all its negative connotations, set up as the 'other' to so-called 'civilised' man, underlines the idea that environment matters to how we are seen. We are partly shaped by where and when we live. But 'modern man', staring at his screens, will not live exuberantly with the Machine by submitting, unthinkingly, to its demands.

How should we live in the world of the Machine? We are clearly intent on finding out, notwithstanding any concerns about the effects of digital technology on the well-being of pupils and staff. Technology is often fetishised in schools as if it is, in itself, a good thing. Many initiatives revolve around the idea that this tablet or this app is going to change our lives for the better, so they are introduced without a second thought. Can we use machines and systems to free ourselves, or do we end up tyrannised by the insistence that our data has to show that we are continually improving? As Allan Bloom (1987: 249) put it: 'The most successful tyranny … is the one that removes the awareness of other possibilities.'

Justin Rosenstein is so aware of the 'bright dings of pseudo-pleasure' that occur when we get a Facebook 'like' that he has become suspicious of their hollow seductivity (Lewis, 2017). Rosenstein is the inventor of what was originally called the 'awesome' button. He says: 'It is very common for humans to develop things with the best of intentions and for them to have unintended, negative consequences.' People have become addicted to their smartphones in such a profound way that they touch their screens thousands of times a day. He adds that there is evidence that cognition and IQ are being affected deleteriously because everyone is being distracted constantly.

Some people, especially those in the education sector, deny that this is a worry. That many are undercover in full sight as fifth columnists, working for the technology sector as Apple, Google and Microsoft Teachers, seems not to be of nearly enough concern in our schools. The reason we are being distracted is that this is exactly what the people who designed the technology intended. Why are you pulled to social media? Why does it keep you in its embrace? Notifications and clickbait headlines are all tuned in to your desires. What's not to like? Your machine is enchanting you. But this is not an equal relationship: an object has objectified man. This is the world of 'persuasive design' – something to play with and, ultimately, to take away our freedom. As Lydia Millet (2009: 23) observes in *How the Dead Dream*: 'The market made a fool of you by giving you what you wanted.'

Big Brother wasn't imposed on us. Instead we continue to spend lots of money inviting him into our homes, so much so that we live permanently in Room 101. 'The thing that is in Room 101 is the worst thing in the world,' wrote George Orwell (2008 [1949]: 296), yet we are under the illusion that the object in our hand is our best techno-friend. We are being broken, not by fear but by the calm inertia of being wedded to the Machine. Our lowest desires are pandered to and we react with anger, shallow 'likes' and instant revulsion, many times a day. But this is not the way to live a good life. These technologies give us what we desire, but the swing and exuberance isn't ours: it belongs to the Machine.

We are human life distracted. If we ever had free will, we have freely given it away to Silicon Valley-based conglomerates. And there are many people who believe that we should go along with this new reality by acquiring what they call '21st century skills'. What this means in practice is that we give up our actual freedom for an illusion of freedom in which we are manipulated (or should that read machine-pulated?) by our smarter-than-us phones. The term '21st century skills' is an oxymoron because, in reality, we are being deskilled.

This is most obvious in the proposal that young people should simply be given the skills to look things up on the internet, to seek out nuggets of knowledge when needed and, rather than be exposed to the grand narratives that an exceptional curriculum can provide, to follow their instincts and curiosities. But these knowledge nuggets, provided by global tech companies, are anathema to those who believe that it is networks of meanings and values that give structure to our lives. Culture isn't provided by search engines; we are more likely to see our worst and most fragmented selves staring back at us in the results of a Google search. Curriculum gives structure to knowledge, and is therefore the first port of call for those of us who are suspicious of a fragmented and child-centred approach. This suggests that curriculum might be more hedgehog than fox. But the point is to provide not one but a variety of ways of making meaning, as opposed to a narrative-free pick 'n' mix.

As we have seen, some, like Mary Midgley (1994: 9), go further with the machine metaphor than simply systems and technology, in thinking of what pupils learn as 'programmes on computers made of meat'. Any knowledge will do to program the meat computer. If we think of learning as simply storing knowledge in the long-term memory files in the brain, then we are ignoring the subjective quality that being a conscious human animal brings to education.

Chapter 5

Input-Output

Science aspires to objectivity … but we need to be wary about what we lose by ignoring the point of view from which we do the observing … Every glance that we cast towards the world is made from a particular perspective.

Carlo Rovelli, *The Order of Time* (2018)

The brain-as-computer suggests that all we need to do is to input knowledge into a child's brain and ensure that it can be retained and retrieved when needed. This mechanistic analogy reduces education to an algorithmic process which results in each child progressing through fixed stages to reach a targeted grade. It is a system that, as Raymond Tallis (2005) puts it, 'eradicates the person' by aspiring to an objective view. It misses the point of education entirely.

Human life (a life in the human realm) is too complex to be summed up as a flight path in which a child's progress through education is trackable on a line chart. An education in the pursuit of wisdom must help children to explore their perspectives, expand their vocabulary and enhance their experiences, so that they might live a life within a number of conversations and within a wide variety of domains. This is where human wisdom is born.

Education is not an input–output model where computers made of meat store readily downloaded information. A curriculum is not a collection of snippets; it is a living and adaptive model through which we can begin to see the vastness and complexity of our shared lives and understandings and join in with the great conversations of all time.

Education is part of the human subjective experience. Education is from someone, somewhere, to someone, somewhere. These 'someones' look upon one another, and at the things being taught and learned, with a viewpoint. The attempt to make education into a purely input–output process overlooks the human as a conscious subject who gazes out onto the world and has an attitude towards the learning. It is important to understand this subjective connection to learning: the perspectives of the teacher and the learners cannot be explained away. They are the very nature of the educative contract. The attention we pay to the act of being informed means that somewhere between the input and the output there is a human feeling, judging, dismissing and/or enjoying. Athena brings the human back in by focusing on more than just knowledge – by looking at how we come to make judgements, how we develop our taste and opinions, how we form our thoughts and points of view, and how we reflect on experiences we have had, experiences we are having and experiences we are yet to have.

As Kevin Mitchell, associate professor of genetics and neuroscience at Trinity College Dublin, puts it: 'even when two people are exposed to what looks objectively like the same environment or circumstances, their subjective experiences may be highly different. And it is the subjective experience that determines whether we learn from something and how it shapes our future behaviour.'

A good curriculum takes into account the subjective nature of the teacher, the pupils and the material being studied and communicated. Curriculum is about artefacts, ideas, works, thoughts and actions being shared. What is taught, to all intents and purposes, 'objectively' is made subjective by the teacher and the pupils. Crucially, what is communicated by the teacher is not necessarily what is thought by the pupil. The artefact or event is described by the subjective teacher to the subjective pupil, who cogitates and understands through a conscious mind and as part of an immediate classroom community. This communication is understood in the context of the particular human beings at this particular time and place, as well as drawing relevance from the universal truths and meanings they might be uncovering.

Asking a pupil a question to find out what they know is not like asking Google (which, somewhat counter-intuitively, doesn't 'know' anything). New knowledge doesn't just find itself slotted into the mind of a child; rather, it comes to be understood by each child differently. It is imbued with their own way of understanding. It is a personal affair, which is then made communal through the social fabric provided by their classmates and the wider school culture. Writing, reading, thinking and doing all play their part.

Instead of input—output machines, human beings are embodied and situated. We are connected to cultural, social, environmental, intellectual and emotional networks, through which we expect certain things to happen in certain ways. We predict things, such as the taste of milk in our tea, and then we are surprised by the novelty of finding out that our predictions are wrong, such as that the milk tastes sour. This is when and how we learn, for example, to check the 'use by' date on the milk carton. And if this new way of seeing seems to fit with the world, then our minds adapt to and, in turn, adapt our environment.

Consider how humans have developed tools, spoken language, written words, cultural artefacts and social practices that impact on us and change our ways of understanding the world and ourselves. If we think of education as simply providing formal knowledge to be stored in our long-term memory, then we ignore the role that experience – provided by the embodied and situated nature of our humanity – has on our ability to be as we might want to be and on how we act in the world. Much of this comes to us through conscious choice, but also through our lives as lived. Our 'experience' is difficult to quantify but this tacit knowledge makes up most of what we know. Art is one way to link us to this knowledge. It can open us up to a world we are barely aware of, and in a way that is sometimes referred to as 'speaking to the heart'. If we were simple computers made of meat, we wouldn't appreciate or make art in the way we do.

As professor of logic and metaphysics Andy Clark (2016: 279) puts it:

Our human-built worlds are not merely the arenas in which we live, work, and play. They also structure the life-long statistical immersions that build and rebuild the generative models that inform each agent's repertoire for perception, action, and reason. By constructing a succession of designer environments, such as the human-built worlds of education, structured play, art, and science, we repeatedly restructure our own minds. These designer environments have slowly become tailored to creatures like us, and they 'know' us as well as we know them. As a species, we refine them again and again, generation by generation. It is this iterative re-structuring, and not sheer processing power, memory, mobility, or even the learning algorithms themselves, that completes the human mental mosaic.

Our world helps us to think and, in turn, our thinking helps to reshape the world. Our minds are not encased in bone but are in a symbiotic relationship with our bodies. Our immediate knowledge webs do not simply exist internally within our brains, but also externally in our social fabric, culture and world. In other words, we are invested in the things that surround us, socially, culturally and technologically, as well as in our memories and internal dialogue.

A computer has no such investment. It doesn't 'know' what it knows. Humans have an awareness of knowing and not-knowing, understanding and misunderstanding. This is the major difference between machine learning and human learning. As human beings, we are aware of the thing we are learning and of the qualitative nature of this awareness. We also have an awareness of how our emotional maturity and/or fragility can affect how we are in the world and how this may be impacting on how well we are learning. Suffice to say, we can be a help or a hindrance to our own learning; between the teacher and the thing-being-learned is the person (the pupil) who is intent on learning, ignoring, misinterpreting or remembering it differently than intended. Learning is inherently subjective. Part of this learning is being-in-the-world; it is how we reach out into the environment and how it shapes us. Arguments that try to decide what is 'best' to include in a curriculum in 'objective' ways are doomed to failure. Most of the why about what to include is entirely subjective and contestable. This is a good thing.

The Mind Is Not a Machine

The fact that we feel we are conscious, subjective beings is regarded, by some, as problematic for science, and this should give us pause for thought. For idealist philosophers, consciousness is the 'hard problem', but there is an alternative argument which suggests that consciousness is a function of the biological machine which has emerged gradually over time. This implies that there is no hard problem at all; consciousness is merely a by-product.

The philosopher Daniel Dennett (1989) believes that humans are like conscious robots, and that one day it might be possible to make a machine that develops consciousness (at this point, he argues, we should grant robots 'personhood'). However, Roger Penrose (1994), Emeritus Rouse Ball professor of mathematics at the University of Oxford, thinks that computers as currently envisaged will not achieve consciousness. For Penrose, computers do not understand – and will never be able to understand – what they are doing or make meaning of the calculations they make. They are mindless; devoid of understanding and judgement.

Alan Turing (1950) asked the question, 'Can machines think?' However, the question that concerns us here is: is *our* mind a machine? If we think of the brain as a computer, the electrical impulses (the neurons) don't 'know' anything when we are thinking. There is simply an input and an output, with nothing of substance in-between. We might have a capacity for memory storage, but this mechanical process is of no interest to 'us' because 'we' don't exist. We are biological machines.

If the mind is a machine, then the answer to Turing's question is yes. If so, the relationship between man and machine is not so fraught; it is merely one of adaptation rather than conquest. The machine that concerns us most is the computer – the thinking or learning machine. Artificial intelligence seems to have gained widespread acceptance, but the outsourcing of intelligence to algorithmic machines represents an interesting quandary for humankind.

When we write words in a notebook, we are downloading our knowledge onto the page, but we don't kid ourselves that the book 'knows' what we have written. The same applies to a computer: it might be a source of information but it doesn't 'know' the information. Similarly, if we give a pocket calculator some instructions and it comes up with an answer, it would not make sense to say that it 'thinks' about it. If I am asked the same question and I can reach no answer (it is an extremely hard sum), but I have been thinking – hard, but ultimately to no avail – I am aware of the struggle. The calculator gets it right with no awareness at all. Thinking is not about getting things right or coming up with a solution. If it were, then machines would be deemed more thoughtful than us humans, at least sometimes.

With the advent of machine learning, do we have to re-examine what learning means? I don't think so. A machine doesn't know what it is to be human, just as I do not know what it is to be a dog. Yet, as I am organic matter, I probably have a closer affinity to my dog than to a machine. My consciousness of my own inevitable demise might set me apart from my dog, but if a machine were to develop consciousness of its potential demise, would it have an existential crisis or would there be an absolute belief in a rebooted afterlife?

If we do create machines that can develop consciousness, will their consciousness be an awareness of being a machine, and therefore a completely different experience to human consciousness? That a machine might one day rival human beings in both intelligence and consciousness does not mean that it is the same thing. Just as a calculator doesn't 'think' in the same way as I do, and a fork lift truck can lift far more weight than I can, this doesn't mean that my mind and body have been usurped. This is obvious, of course, but what is crucial is the 'I' that makes it so. What is this 'I' to which I am referring? What is it that makes me, well, me? It is my awareness of *my* difference to the dog, the calculator and the fork lift truck that is central.

Consciousness seems to have no reason to exist in evolutionary terms. Some philosophers argue that it doesn't exist at all and is merely an illusion (though who or what is fooled by this illusion is left begging). Others suggest that consciousness is all there is and that reality is a feature of consciousness. Neither option seems to offer us a satisfactory solution. Whatever the truth is, we are all aware of being conscious and it has meaning in our lives. It seems to be an experience that is 'outside' of being a biological machine.

If we regard the mind as a machine, albeit a complex one, then education becomes pure programming and we should work out how to do it as efficiently as possible. But what if the mind isn't a machine? If the mind is not synonymous with the brain, then curriculum is not simply a means of knowledge uploading. It would be much easier if it was …

If our schools are run entirely on cold pseudo-objectivity, then we have crossed a line. If objectivity becomes our master, to the exclusion of other points of view, then education is bereft of multiple ways of seeing, thinking and understanding. Human beings flourish because we see things in different ways. Truth is only experienced if we stay open to the multitude of perspectives that lead to it.

Chapter 6
The Teacher

How much of the role of the teacher has become objective and rationalised? If this aspect of teaching is being increased at the expense of the subjective and intuitive, is there a loss? How much of teaching is a science and how much of it is an art?

As cogs in the bureaucratic Machine, teachers are required to be rational and efficient. In the classroom, they are expected to be professional, which means performing tasks deemed to be essential to the smooth running of the organisation and ensuring that pupils progress towards a predetermined target. This target is a final grade, added to which might be a destination and a salaried career (or 'social mobility'). Thus, the teacher is the front-line instrument of social engineering and the producer of highly graded individuals. The teacher is no longer a teacher of their subject, a purveyor of wisdom, but rather a salesperson of pathways.

The teacher is judged by the grades of those in their charge. They are required to pursue target data and pass these targets on to their charges. The teacher is instructed to use technology to 'improve the education' of their pupils, but how this is to be done is not made clear. Education churns out numbers and neglects wisdom.

According to research by the Liberal Democrats, during the academic year 2016/2017 there were 3,750 teachers on long-term leave suffering from stress. This represented an increase of 5% since the previous year. The figures make clear the 'impossible pressures' that teachers are under, a situation which is exacerbated by the teacher recruitment crisis and an obsession with exam results (Bloom, 2018). When people feel they are not in control, they become stressed. Excel spreadsheets and emails dominate far too much of a teacher's time. The pupils (rows on a spreadsheet) are reduced to numbers which progress through a series of levels. If they slip back here, we adjust the education dose there.

In a discussion with Sam Harris, Professor Jordan B. Peterson, the controversial clinical psychologist from the University of Toronto, suggested: 'The thing about the scientific viewpoint is that it leaves certain things out and it leaves out what it doesn't know … it also looks at the world in a particular way … for example, it strips the world of its subjectivity.' Harris replied: 'There is nothing about my conception of science that discounts the reality or the significance of subjectivity … I have ridden that same hobbyhorse against that conception of science myself' (Harris, 2017: 44 mins). The scientific materialist view can denigrate both humankind and science.

Harris does not seem to support a materialist view, nor does he deny that 'the mind could play any role in determining the character of reality'. Human beings understand the world – the nature of reality – through the filter of the conscious mind. It is within this subjective world that the teacher does their job. In *Consciousness: A User's Guide*, Adam Zeman (2004: 341) states: 'Dualism respects our belief that experience is special, but leaves the interaction of mind and matter deeply mysterious. Physicalism, which tries to redescribe experience in one or other kind of physical vocabulary, explains how mind can trade with matter, but does so by cheating our … intuition – and "leaving out the mind".'

If we take the mechanistic approach, we 'leave out the mind'; and if we reject the mechanical approach then we are left with that which is deeply mysterious. Both approaches are unsatisfactory. The teacher must be cognisant of the mechanical and the mysterious (the subjective mind): the science of teaching and the art of teaching. In the classroom, the teacher has a moment in time to be, and to be in communion with the pupils as they really are (or envisage themselves to be). The human beings existing in that moment are ready to experience a lesson through their conscious subjective minds.

The mechanistic approach pressurises teachers to forget this. It tries to objectify the subjective relationship at the heart of teaching. This relationship – the essential communion between teacher and pupil – is one of storyteller/conversationalist with another who is yet to be brought into the story and the conversation. Listening, knowing, thinking, caring, conversing and speaking are at the heart of the story. Being-in-the-classroom is about caring for the class, the story and the moment. Instead of breaking things down, it brings things together.

We need to care about this space more than anything else in the school. Instead of everything bearing down on the teacher and their pupils, we should build up everything from the teacher and their pupils. This is where the story and our engagement with it begins to unfold. Both teacher and pupils are thrown into this space which is full of possibility. The teacher is part of the story they are telling and the pupils react to the story, to the teacher and to each other. When the story is working well, when everything is flowing, then in all likelihood we forget any distinctions and get lost in the moment. It is only when something goes wrong – the chalk breaks, the tech fails, a wasp flies in through an open window, the teacher spills their coffee, a pupil farts loudly – that we become aware of the relationships around us.

This is the world described by Heidegger as *Dasein* (which means 'presence' or 'being-in-the-world'). Firstly, we are attuned: we are historical beings, aware of our place in a space, and we react to it. Secondly, it is discursive: we articulate and interpret through our shared language and culture. Thirdly, it is understanding which makes sense of our being there. This is the teacher teaching in the classroom. It is past, present, future; it is grammar, dialectic, rhetoric (see Robinson, 2013).

To reiterate: the art of teaching means the teacher being a teacher and the pupil being a pupil, from which all else follows – and not the other way round. It is mind, body, voice, chalk, board, book, paper, pencil and ears – in a variety of combinations and directions – and the teacher needs to be free to be first and foremost 'the person who teaches' within this space. The classroom should be a place where we can find respite from the Machine. The classroom is the place where conversations around the qualitative curriculum take place. One of the qualities this curriculum must communicate is what makes something 'good'.

Good Books

What is a 'good' book? When we teach a book, it is never going to be the same for everyone who reads it. In the teacher's reality, informed by the canon and their connoisseurship, it is a good book, so their job is to help their pupils recognise why a good book is good – what it is that makes it so. But they can only take this so far. Eventually, there comes the point when the teacher must leave the pupils to make the ultimate decision of whether it is good for them. A key part of education is becoming free of the teacher.

A completely materialistic viewpoint would suggest that a book can be 'proven' to be good through scientific method, independently of human judgement. For example, Renaissance UK carried out some research using a 'readability formula' to ascertain a text's complexity, scoring each book between 0.2 and 13.5. While they admit that 'No scientific formula can take into consideration the maturity of the themes addressed or the sophistication of the literary devices employed by the author', they still managed to give *Mr Greedy* by Roger Hargreaves a book level of 4.4 and John Steinbeck's Pulitzer Prize-winning *The Grapes of Wrath* 4.9 (Flood, 2019).

While we might enjoy both books, especially at different ages, this numerical approach shows certain limitations. We could question their algorithm or their intent, but *The Grapes of Wrath* is clearly not 0.5 more complex than *Mr Greedy*. This sort of judgement is meaningless: *The Grapes of Wrath* is arguably much more complex than *Mr Greedy*. Numbers don't help us here – only subjective viewpoints can. Can we really accept a 'readability' and 'complexity' judgement that is decided by science rather than by readers? And if we can, do we give the science more credence than our own judgement? Is the 'readability formula' more wise than we? The very thing the formula is unable to capture – the maturity of themes and sophistication of literary devices – is precisely the point where the human being interacts with the book. Although it is common for online bookstores like Amazon to convince us to rank books out of five, some of us still feel that human judgement is more sophisticated than a number can ever convey. If the difference of 0.5 between *Mr Greedy* and *The Grapes of Wrath* is absurd, let's not start on grading children's writing over a whole year using just one number.

A non-materialist view would argue that the pupil is completely free to decide whether a book is good or not, and also to decide whether they wish to read it or not. They might stick with this immature decision, and like the spoilt child who won't eat broccoli or Brussels sprouts, might never appreciate the bitter tastes that are the sign of a more sophisticated palate.

Both of these stances negate the role of the teacher because they regard the human (subjective) perspective as secondary. In both cases, the teacher could be replaced by a machine. But if we value the position of the teacher as a human being, then beauty is in the eye of the beholder and in the object being seen. This is the teacher's unique role – they help the pupil to understand why an object is beautiful, so that the pupil might say: 'I can see this beauty' or 'I understand this beauty.' And then the teacher gives them the ability to go further: 'But to me it is not beautiful because …' or 'It is beautiful because …' or, sometimes, 'It has qualities I can't quite grasp …' That is, to articulate an understanding of both the historical object and the subjective perspective of taste, aesthetic awareness and discrimination.

The danger here is in making one opinion equal to any other opinion. Relativism is flawed: everything is reduced to a valueless free-for-all in which all morality, opinions and truths have equal worth/worthlessness. It is the teacher's job to educate their pupils' palates. There is a risk that by acknowledging that their pupils have a range of thoughts, tastes and opinions, the teacher is swayed into believing that these opinions are all of equivalent worth and so should be expressed equally freely. The philistine can call great art shit and the racist can opine on immigration, but this is not the teacher's job. In the classroom, the only opinions worth exploring are educated opinions. The teacher's task is to help pupils navigate this subjective world. The teacher needs to understand the complexities behind what they are teaching, why and when, and then pay sufficient attention to the pupils' understanding of what they are being taught. The teacher needs to teach about values and meanings, beautiful things and ugly things, ideas that go beyond the facts – and which can be seen in context of the great conversations of our own time and, indeed, of all time.

The teacher needs to care enough to find out whether the pupils understand what things might be beautiful and true, and why. Have their pupils developed the capacity to appreciate things which initially they found to be distasteful or lacking in meaning? Have they developed trust in their teacher's judgement because they know that one day they will fully understand why this judgement might add to or even become their own? The curriculum story needs to matter to the teacher teaching it in order for it to matter to the children learning it.

The teacher's job is to negotiate the truth with varying degrees of certainty and bring the pupil to the point of recognition about what it is to be themselves within these different realms of truth: to be opened to truth and to be able to negotiate it in their lives. The teacher must not tolerate the destructive get-out clause: 'It's my opinion, and therefore I won't be challenged ...' The teacher must make things manifest to their pupils in the subjective space and give them an awareness that it is an ever-changing space in which truth and beauty can be found.

Teaching to the Test

The office school might decree that lesson plans are checked by line managers, that they are designed in three parts, that books must be marked and up to date, that pupils must be seen to be engaged. When it comes to the curriculum, the main concern is what to include to get the highest grades, even if this means teaching children easier texts, fewer great ideas and leaving them without an overview as to how the world works, might work or could work.

High grades (or at least 'on target' grades) trump a high quality education. This means that pupils are assessed on exam criteria from day one. The whole focus of their schooling is on an exam that might be five years away. Pupils are taught a limited number of texts, concepts and ideas in order to prepare them for the types of answers expected in the final exam. Aspects of the exam might provide excellent teaching points, but the mechanics of the exam should not influence the curriculum. I have worked with schools which teach the same texts again and again to children all the way through from age 11 to 18 because they appear at GCSE and A level. They are also taught how to write about them in 'exam speak', answering for a 2-pointer, a 16-pointer and so on.

This is what a mechanical curriculum looks like in practice. Subjects aren't included for their fundamental worth but because they 'facilitate' other subjects – those subjects which top universities apparently value above the rest. Texts aren't selected for their quality but for their likelihood to deliver results. Children aren't regarded as human beings with a right to be well educated but as customers purchasing a clutch of grades that make the school look good, and that the young person can trade in for more of the same at another institution.

The commodification of curriculum in this way is not wise.

… at the very heart of education sits the vast accumulated wealth of human knowledge and what we choose to impart to the next generation: the curriculum.

Without a curriculum, a building full of teachers, leaders and pupils is not a school. Without receiving knowledge, pupils have learned nothing and no progress has been made – whatever the measures might indicate. This is why exams should exist in the service of the curriculum rather than the other way round. Exams are our best measure of what has been successfully transmitted to the pupil's cognition. We must not forget, however, that any test can only ever sample the knowledge that has been gained. It is the whole domain that is of matter to the pupil. (Ofsted and Spielman, 2017)

We need to free the teacher and rid ourselves of restrictions to learning. We need to take away bureaucracy from the classroom. Remove the business model of deliverology. Cast aside the tick-boxing layers of middle management. So much expertise, based on so little, for the benefit of so few …

The task ahead is to ensure that pupils are initiated into the great conversation, that they engage intellectually, physically and spiritually with the journey towards wisdom and begin worshipping at the feet of Athena. The teacher, divested of mere data-gathering tasks, needs to become the focus of the school, joining a collective of subject experts who are free to become involved in the world of academe or art, plying their skills as part of a tradition, participating in a conversation that has continued through the ages.

Chapter 7

Performance Management

... we don't need neuroscience to tell us why the annual performance review song-and-dance is so universally reviled. We have our own reasons: the endless paperwork, the evaluation criteria so utterly unrelated to our jobs, and the simplistic and quota-driven ratings used to label the performance of otherwise complex, educated human beings.

Jena McGregor,
The Corporate Kabuki of Performance Reviews (2013)

Employers are also finally acknowledging that both supervisors and subordinates despise the appraisal process – a perennial problem that feels more urgent now that the labor market is picking up and concerns about retention have returned.

Peter Cappelli and Anna Tavis,
The Performance Management Revolution (2016)

In *Eichmann in Jerusalem: A Report on the Banality of Evil*, Hannah Arendt (2006 [1963]) writes: 'the nature of every bureaucracy, is to make functionaries and mere cogs in the administrative machinery out of men, and thus to dehumanize them'. When places of education shift from being about the pursuit of wisdom into being accumulators of data, it is inevitable that the pupil ceases to be part of the enquiry and ends up being judged on where they appear on a spreadsheet. By treating schools as businesses and children as customers, we end up trying to keep the customers happy and delivering what they want.

The intrusion of the workplace into all aspects of a teacher's life is not to be welcomed. Never being able to switch off mentally, and the guilt when they do so physically, is not conducive to well-being. Allied to this is the creeping

Taylorism of the school, where positive business practices are seen as yet another way to 'solve' the problem that is education. Frederick Taylor aimed to increase productivity by improving efficiency through what he termed 'scientific management', including the use of time and motion studies, the deskilling of the worker and the increased control of managers.

Nowadays, top-down managerialism checks on and controls more and more of the day-to-day existence of staff. That a school is not a business, and that efficiency isn't necessarily achievable in the same way that it might be in a factory, seems to have passed some people by. The myriad daily decisions made by a teacher can be honed and improved, but trying to accomplish this in a Taylorist way works against the very thing that can achieve these aims successfully. An experienced teacher works more quickly and effectively than the data-heavy systems which try to over-measure everything that is needed to track a dumbed-down workforce.

Nevertheless, the education system continues to ape the business world, no more so than in the idea of the 'effective manager'. All it takes is one read of Stephen Covey's *The Seven Habits of Highly Effective People* (2004) and a day course on leadership, and the effective manager is full of the latest jargon to improve *you*. One of the ways they do this is through performance management, which has all of the characteristics of machine thinking and all of the limitations. So limited is it, in fact, that businesses like Accenture, Deloitte and Microsoft are abandoning performance management in their droves (Cunningham, 2015b).

In recent times, there has been a huge increase in middle management – leadership became all the rage. Some were even given special monikers, such as 'advanced skills leader' or 'leader of learning'. This vast increase in the bureaucracy within schools – and, simultaneously, the individual peccadilloes of individual managers – meant that the poor bloody infantry often didn't understand what they were meant to be doing, apart from getting more adept at obfuscation when filling in forms. A culture of second-guessing what was wanted by management also developed. This entailed trying to ascertain who were the 'important' and 'less important' chiefs. Thus, performance management became focused on rewards for compliance and punishment for non-compliance. It also became easier to bully employees, in subtle – and sometimes not so subtle – ways.

But is performance management as useful as some people claim? The head of Accenture, Pierre Nanterme, said: 'We are not sure that spending all that time on performance management has been yielding such a great outcome' (Cunningham, 2015a). Many companies report that it is time-consuming and has the opposite effect to the one desired. Instead of motivating employees, it encourages disengagement and restricts their ability to improve: 'Brain research has shown that even employees who get positive reviews experience negative effects from the process' (Cunningham, 2015b).

How many hours have you spent trying to justify that you have fulfilled your targets, often targets you had completely forgotten about during the year and only recalled during a review or appraisal? This realisation should ring alarm bells. Yet schools embrace target setting to help them justify performance-related pay increases and other similarly corrosive ways of dividing and ruling their staff.

Teachers need to be given the freedom to grow – and I don't mean that old management trick of giving them enough rope to hang themselves. Freedom should be about nurturing and building strong supportive relationships throughout the school. It should be about encouraging openness: no closed classrooms, no big event reviews, just conversations between professionals. This is a far more effective way of encouraging the informal professionalism that can drive dynamic organisations.

It is not just staff who are subjected to such nonsense. In classrooms up and down the country, children are subjected to third-rate performance management targets and appraisals which take up a huge amount of lesson time. 'Big data – give us lots of data!' is the cry. Managers justify their pay scale by chasing teachers for data, more data! Instead of teaching and learning, a bureaucratic monstrosity in the name of improving performance is inflicted on pupils in an attempt to prepare them for the 21st century skill of wasting time in pointless form filling.

Here is what every teacher should do to resist this peculiar pastime:

- Stop setting target grades for your children.

- Stop setting meaningless target statements.

- Stop children from wasting their time reviewing the targets that you have set for them or that they have set for themselves.

Instead:

- Spend the time saved by teaching, supporting and nurturing pupils so they can understand more.

These simple steps might annoy a line manager or two, but they will probably help your pupils more.

The best way of acquiring feedback on what to do, how to improve and how to change is through day-to-day interactions with colleagues. Time is far better spent observing each other's work – not formally, just sharing ideas, having a coffee or breaking bread together. Much more is going to get done well with our pupils when we are working as a team to design and deliver a great curriculum. Instead of forever focusing on 'Is this teacher any good?', the question should be 'Is the curriculum any good?' If we concentrate on this, rather than on veiled threats and possible rewards, and if we develop staff by improving the curriculum, then the resulting positivity will infect the school.

A focus on curriculum design brings together professional teams for a common purpose. There are also moments throughout the year when departments and teams can take stock, such as the end of a school year, when exam results come through or after the school play or carol concert. These natural rhythms will vary from school to school, but teams can use these moments to reflect: does our school bureaucracy work for the wisdom of all?

The machine of bureaucracy – like other machines – is designed to make things, but instead of churning out cars it churns out rules and diktats. And, most notably, instead of being regarded as human beings, those who work in the institution are thought of as human resources – and resources, like any tool or technology, exist for the good of the institution and are measurable and disposable. The rules and diktats are the oil that runs the Machine. The pupils are resources too, hopefully supplying useful data for the ultimate good of the office school. The Machine's manipulation of behaviour and performance lacks meaning for the individuals concerned, except in a shallow way: responding to data on a spreadsheet as if it tells a greater truth than that involved in day-to-day interactions and judgements.

In *John Dewey, Confucius and Global Philosophy*, Joseph Grange (2004: 31–32) writes about how a dystopian future might make itself apparent:

> Meaning would fade away and be replaced by data. The responsibility to carry out human judgment … would be traded in for the security of statistical analysis. Numbers would be substituted for argument and reason. Machines would make irrefutable decisions. Human beings would become resources to be quantified. Life would flatten out and intensity, depth, and width of experience would be lost.

Argument, reason, judgement, subjective thought and discussion can all be informed by data, but they cannot be replaced by them. If we don't know what the data is telling us, we need to face up to that truth. We need to learn to see beyond the data – what it is not telling us as well as what it is. We need to decide what data is necessary and useful, and develop the skill of dealing with this information honestly.

Chapter 8

Science and Scientism

Computers are by far the best metaphor for lots of things ... we are robot survival machines, and because genes themselves can't pick things up, catch things, eat things, or run around, they have to do that by proxy; they have to build machines to do it for them. That is us.

Richard Dawkins, A Survival Machine (1996)

It is ... often seen as scientific to talk as if people were ... machines. This machine imagery has been so useful ... that many people no longer think of it as a metaphor but as a scientific fact.

Mary Midgley, *The Myths We Live By* (2004)

Schools are being urged to apply 'what works' to their systems and to their teaching and learning. Indeed, it would be madness to apply the opposite: 'what doesn't work' is not something that would motivate teachers and pupils in a grand coalition to cultivate ignorance.

Governments around the world are coming round to the importance of applying cognitive science to education. At a teaching conference in 2017, England's schools minister, Nick Gibb, said that teachers should 'pursue well-evidenced teaching methods' and 'have up-to-date knowledge of cognitive science and the implications for what and how to teach'. Cognitive science grew from the disciplines of psychology, neuroscience, linguistics, anthropology and, significantly for my argument here, artificial intelligence and computer programming. This means that the computational and mechanistic metaphor is right at the centre of contemporary thinking about how schools should teach and how pupils should learn. It embodies the idea that materialist science can solve all the mysteries of life, the universe and everything, and leads us to a point of view where all other ways to truth are either not exact enough to warrant being called 'truths' or are illusory. If this is so, and our endeavours in schooling are truly about wisdom and truth seeking, then we might as well give up teaching most subjects: they are so lost to truth that we cannot justify their inclusion in the curriculum.

If this science is correct, then are human beings computers made of meat? If the answer is yes, then this might partly explain why the school as a machine moves so easily from metaphor to fact. How can we use science to help education rather than dominate it?

Mary Midgley describes how machine imagery became useful for science in the 17th century when the 'clockwork' model was applied to the solar system. Later, when the Industrial Revolution took hold, the metaphor became even more entrenched. That physics has now abandoned the mechanical model, because of the complexity found at a sub-atomic level, doesn't mean that the metaphor has been abandoned throughout all of science. It is still common thinking for those who believe that we should take a more scientific approach towards what happens in schools.

Scientific research is an important tool. It can provide a valuable way of understanding how best to educate children – for example, how we learn to read and retain information. However, the idea that science is the *only* way to inform education is a reductive one. Quantum physicist David Deutsch argues that reductionism is a mistake (2011: 124). He rejects the idea that scientific knowledge consists of a hierarchy of explanations, and believes instead that any level of explanation can be fundamental. Art, philosophy, biology and physics can all offer fundamental explanations. Science does not have the only true insights into our world and experiences.

Qualia and Scientism

A curriculum as straightforward input–output is very different to a curriculum which takes account of pupils as individuals with a range of views and perspectives. Surely, our subjective consciousness of what we are learning about impacts on the quality of that learning?

Much of the work that takes place in schools is in the subjective realm (our consciousness of the world) – indeed, we talk about the 'culture' of a school. This is the world that, as human beings, we understand more implicitly than any other. Curriculum is wholly within this world. Yet it is also the world that science knows the least. This is not to say that science will never understand the subjective realm, but it is a long way from doing so. Yet, even if it did, would its understanding be akin to our experiences as individuals in the world? Some might argue that consciousness is irrelevant to teaching and learning, or a minor inconvenience to the job of knowledge transferral, but think about it … If you are thinking about it, either for or against the argument I'm making, or degrees in-between, isn't your consciousness of this fact relevant?

Can education be an entirely objective process? Schools were developed around the idea that we are conscious beings with free will, subjective thoughts, tastes and characteristics. 'Qualia' is the term used by philosophers to describe the introspective, subjective aspects of our mental lives – for example, how we experience the redness of red. We might well be mechanistic beings who have developed consciousness, but even so, our consciousness is real to us: we experience qualia.

As a materialist, Daniel Dennett (1991) rebuts the idea that qualia exist. He grants that we have conscious experiences but not that these have particularly special qualities. He argues that consciousness has developed genetically and culturally through memetic selection, mainly language. David Deutsch (2011: 154) rejects this theory, suggesting that it is a bad explanation to simply say that qualia 'don't exist'. He believes that we do have qualia but we struggle to describe them. The controversial biologist Rupert Sheldrake (2012: 108–111) suggests that Dennett resorts to materialism due to his insistence that dualism (seeing the body and mind as separate) is wrong. Sheldrake agrees that Cartesian dualism is erroneous – but, he contends, so is materialism.

Others argue that the subjective world of our consciousness is beyond the purview of science because it is subjective. They maintain that science overreaches itself when it attempts to explain away our experience of self and culture through objective measures. This overreaching is often called scientism. The accusation of scientism is usually brought into play to prevent the potential destruction of other areas of knowing that science potentially has within its grasp. Defined in the *Oxford English Dictionary* as 'excessive belief in the power of scientific knowledge and techniques',[1] scientism knows no bounds. Dennett dismisses scientism as a term used by those who have no arguments left and so resort to abuse. However, in *Darwin's Dangerous Idea* (1995: 21) he argues: 'There is no such thing as philosophy-free science; there is only science whose philosophical baggage is taken on board without examination.'

It is the examination of philosophical baggage that I wish to explore here. Dennett is a philosopher, after all, and philosophy isn't science. This hints that there is space for a different approach. Despite Stephen Hawking's declaration that philosophy is dead (Reisz, 2015), Dennett's comment suggests that philosophy does have an important role. For example, if we tried to get rid of philosophy in our understanding of politics and replaced it with science, our political activity would be very different. Marxism might be an example of scientism – Engels was wont to call Marxism a science. Scientists might recoil at this, suggesting that Marxism is, at best, a pseudoscience. But this shows us the problem. Can political philosophy ever be understood by science? Is there one true theory which could show us the best way to organise society? Can our understanding of political philosophy be enhanced by science? The latter grants a smaller role to science but it is also one that accepts its limitations. I'm not sure I would want to live in a society governed entirely by objective science, and neither would I want to work in a school governed in that way. It might be efficient, but would it be humane?

Arguably, what most makes us human is the quality of our knowing – our consciousness of self. Computers can 'know' but they are not conscious. The scientist Roger Penrose argues that the computational model will never explain consciousness. However, he does believe that science may one day understand consciousness – if it rejects current ways of knowing in this field: 'Within that straightjacket, there can be no scientific role for intentionality and subjective experience … a unity with the workings of

---

1   See https://en.oxforddictionaries.com/definition/scientism.

nature is potentially present within all of us, and is revealed in our very faculties of conscious comprehension and sensitivity' (Penrose, 1994: 420). Whether the problem of consciousness is hard or simple, our experience of ourselves is not mechanical. We believe we have a soul, a mind, a consciousness. Call it what you will, our faculties of conscious comprehension and sensitivity are ways to discover great truths about the world and ourselves, and this suggests that different ways of knowing and understanding are important to schooling.

Even those who assert that they don't possess these things in reality believe, to some extent, in the illusion that makes it *seem* real. That these ideas might be problematic, or even irrelevant, doesn't stop us from feeling that they matter. If some scientists prefer to regard subjectivity as unscientific, it doesn't alter the fact that subjectivity is as much a part of their lives as it is for the rest of us.

But this raises a question: if consciousness is an illusion – if we are tricked by conscious subjective understandings and what underpins us is objective and can only be explained objectively – then what part of us is it that is so easily deluded? No amount of knowing how consciousness works objectively will change our experience of how it feels. Curriculum – how we select it and how it is experienced – is very much part of how we see the world and ourselves, much of which takes place in the conscious realm. Curriculum offers us perspectives on coming to terms with ourselves, so having a variety of ways to help us understand our conscious selves is one of its most important insights.

The missing piece of the curriculum jigsaw, for those schools in which a list of topics or copious amounts of knowledge is 'organised' into a rational schema for pupils to learn, is the space for human understanding and judgement, subjectivity and consciousness. In *The Mind of God: Science and the Search for Ultimate Meaning*, Paul Davies, professor of natural philosophy at the University of Adelaide, suggests that just because beliefs 'are held irrationally does not mean they are wrong. Perhaps there is a route to knowledge … that bypasses human reason' (Davies, 1993: 24–25). Is irrationality a good thing? I'm not sure I can argue that it is, but what if good or true things are arrived at irrationally? Some people suggest that religious faith can open up the doors to a 'good life'. There is even some scientific evidence that people who have 'belief' lead happier lives than those without (Chen and VanderWeele, 2018).

In schools, when the evidence is clear it should inform practice, but what of other areas of schooling where 'what works' is an irrelevant or impossible enquiry? Are our rituals, feelings, intuitions, art, humanity and culture as truthful and as important, or just a bunch of superstitions waiting around to be debunked by science? Davies says that he wants to explore human reasoning as far as it can go, and so he should. We should not call for a limit to scientific enquiry. But neither should we call for a limit on other ways of knowing by calling them unscientific and therefore unworthy of attention – unless we want to see the end of all art.

The philosophy of education we adhere to guides the decisions we make. If we approach education from a purely scientific point of view, do we take note of the subjective way in which the science is framed? For example, here is a passage from an article titled 'Music Education Key to Raising Literacy and Numeracy Standards' from Australia's *Sunday Morning Herald*:

Children who undertake formal, ongoing musical education have significantly higher levels of cognitive capacity, specifically in their language acquisition and numerical problem solving skills. They also continue in education for longer, reverse the cognitive issues related to disadvantage and earn and contribute more on average across their lifetime. (Collins, 2015)

And from a chapter about the relationship between emotion and art in *Brain Science for Principals: What School Leaders Need to Know*, Patricia Valente (2016: 89) writes:

Mirror neurons have been found to play a key role in developing self-awareness and social connection ... Drama appears to mirror neurons ... The actor's development of attention and concentration cultivates the capacity to be aware of feelings.

I am not going to argue with the science in these two examples; the science may well be correct. The overreach occurs in the idea that music and drama should be justified in these ways at all. I am questioning the philosophy. Music and drama are both art forms that have been around (and part of education) for longer than science has been 'science', and yet here are two authors attempting to justify the arts in scientific terms. We are being told that music can make children better at literacy and numeracy and that drama cultivates their capacity to be emotionally aware.

If these were simply two rare examples I wouldn't be concerned, but this approach is becoming more prevalent in schools: certain subjects, especially the arts, are justified in the curriculum only if they make children better at an academic subject or improve well-being or brain capacity in some way. The study of music in order to make children better at music and drama to make them better at drama should be argument enough. I think it might be a long time before we find out that the study of maths makes you a better dancer, simply because this question is unlikely to be asked.

The philosopher Michael Oakeshott (1962: 202) writes:

... all that is to be heard is the eristic tones of the voice of science ... an established monopoly will not only make it difficult for another voice to be heard, but it will also make it seem proper that it should not be heard; it is convicted in advance of irrelevance ... it may gain entrance [only] by imitating the voices of monopolists.

The dominant voice of science means that all other ways of seeing the world have to justify their existence in education by demonstrating how they help other subjects further up the academic hierarchy or how they benefit the brain. Studying a subject for its own worth is no longer good enough, unless that subject is mathematics, science or literacy. Of course, science hasn't always been the leading voice in education. During the classical era of Western civilisation, philosophy was the source of truth and dominated educational approaches. This was later replaced by theology – God was in our heads. According to C. P. Snow (1998 [1964]), literature and classics were the next dominant era, but these approaches to truth have now been supplanted by science.

Today, if we want to know what the truth is, our ultimate guide is a scientist rather than a philosopher or a priest. And this is just as true for schooling as it is for any other pursuit. By dropping theology and philosophy, we seem to believe that we have reached a sophisticated point in our history and can look at the foolishness of those from the past who were ignorant of our more enlightened ways. This extreme view of the scientific age is akin to the end of the history of ideas.

Mechanistic Man

The mechanistic approach provides an answer to how we organise our schools, teach our children and design a curriculum, which is why it is prevalent in many institutions:

When schools began assessing people according to precise marks, the lives of millions of students and teachers changed dramatically … the skills required to get high marks in an exam are not the same as a true understanding of literature etc. But when forced to choose between the two, most schools go for the marks. (Harari, 2017: 170)

Precision marking is not the best way to assess an education – as Yuval Noah Harari says, it is 'true understanding' that is vital. But the search for the right science in order to get the right grades continues apace. Science can show us how to get high grades; high grades show us that a successful education has been achieved. According to Cathy O'Neil (2016: 52–53), this is where the science of education reaches its zenith: 'they picked prox-ies that seemed to correlate with success. They looked at SATs scores ... a vicious feedback loop materialized ... the reputational ecosystem ... was overshadowed by a single column of numbers.'

The Machine works in the following way: human organisation is mechan-ical; the human mind is mechanical; education is mechanical. It is all predictable and measurable. We denigrate the validity of our teaching on the basis of the reliability of our measures. If the pursuit of wisdom was the central concern for schools, then we would be worshipping at the feet of Athena and not at the feet of the Machine. The teacher's own pursuit of wisdom should always be an element of the educative process. Not just teaching what is known and what is thought to be known, but also ventur-ing into the unknown and different ways of knowing.

Is Knowledge Enough?

Isaiah Berlin looks to Tolstoy, who compares the 'fanatical theorists [who] bedevil education' with the old-fashioned village priest:

... he treated his pupils as human beings, not as scientists treat specimens in a laboratory; he did what he could; he was often corrupt, ill-tempered, unjust, but these were human – 'natural' – vices, and therefore their effects, unlike those of machine-made modern instructors, inflicted no permanent injury. (Berlin, 2008 [1977]: 241)

What if we viewed education, rather than being a problem to solve, as something living and humane? A humane education is one that nurtures a sense of who 'we' might be-in-the-world. Our understanding of self and world is centred in our conscious awareness. Let us give this type of education a reason: the pursuit of wisdom. We've given it the name Athena because she is the goddess of wisdom. This humane education is self-regulating and dynamic – it shares this with all living things. Wisdom is attained through our dealings with the ordinary and the extraordinary. Understanding comes at the edges of order and chaos, light and darkness, rational and irrational. All life is here. School should include experiences which give children glimpses of thoughts, ideas, emotions and feelings beyond their (of necessity) limited horizons. It should give them the wherewithal to take part, to make choices, to understand, to be free to think, to explore, to test their values and to find meaning in their lives.

The pursuit of wisdom is encapsulated by the quality of experience, the breadth and depth of knowledge and the qualitative nature of the judgements made – that is, curriculum. A curriculum of quality is captured in the idea of great books and other artefacts and ideas of cultural importance. What is great is difficult and controversial to determine. It is shaped by our human values. A curriculum must emphasise the qualitative and subjective nature of the choices being made by emphasising the clash of values as well as the merit of a range of different individual thoughts and experiences. Beyond knowledge, the curriculum should also provide ways of making meaning. It is therefore through values, experiences and meaning-making that it should be organised. This points us towards the idea of a knowledge-rich curriculum. But a knowledge-rich curriculum has to start from the premise that knowledge alone is not enough. We also have to bring the human back in.

Part II

Athena

Chapter 9

Bringing the Human Back In

A knowledge-rich curriculum has to be a human-rich curriculum. Curriculum is our way of helping children look out into the world as conscious, perceiving, thinking and questioning human beings who are able to act upon and within the world, taking care and responsibility of it and each other. How we bring the subjective human back to being the central concern for schooling is through an unyielding focus on curriculum.

Exuberant humans in a scientific age have their own way of experiencing the world. The more thoughtful the articulation of these experiences, the richer the world can seem to those who live in it. Poetry, art and music are ways of knowing and interpreting our world. By being versed in a rich curriculum, a child can begin to fully appreciate the world into which they have been thrown. Sometimes a song knows more about us than a fact about how the brain works does.

In order to bring the human back into the picture, education has to deal with a number of issues which are controversial to, or beyond, current scientific understanding. Chief among these are consciousness (which was discussed in Chapter 8), free will (discussed on page 79) and other theories about what makes us human. A mechanical approach to education fails to deal with these three areas. It is also difficult from an evidence-based perspective because the science isn't conclusive. Yet every day we all experience an impression of being-in-the-world – feelings that we associate with being aware and making choices – which would suggest that it is necessary to take this into account in an educational situation.

Bringing the human back in also opens us up to the most important issue for a knowledge-rich education: our ideas about what should be included in the curriculum are shaped by our subjective and qualitative values about what is important to us as human beings.

The wonderful Jacob Bronowski wrote that we have used science 'as a machine without will'. He aspired to unity between the sciences and the arts, and believed that this could be achieved by 'looking into the human personality' and 'explor[ing] what makes him man' (Bronowski, 2008 [1951]: 153). Curriculum design is a subjective action that belongs to the world as humankind experiences it. We make decisions about what to include and how to communicate it, making difficult choices through feelings, argument and reason. Teachers and pupils face each other in the classroom not as data points but as living, breathing, conscious beings. The curriculum is the major way in which we can help children to make sense of what it is to be thoughtful animals in a dynamic world. This is the essence of what is meant by knowledge-rich – how we are conscious of the world and our place within it.

In *Ideas: A History of Thought and Invention, from Fire to Freud*, Peter Watson (2005: 1015) says:

Science has proved an enormous success in regard to the world 'out there' but has so far failed in the one area that arguably interests us the most – ourselves. Despite the general view that the self arises in some way from brain activity ... it is hard to escape the conclusion that, after all these years, we still don't know even how to talk about consciousness, about the self.

It is not a crazy notion to ask for a mutually respectful space in which different ways of knowing can exist side by side, and that all are given equal credence in helping us to find our place in the world. This entails both objective and subjective ways of seeing, bearing in mind that theories from the subjective realm lead us into doubt and uncertainty but, arguably, no more so than those from the objective realm.

Other Ways of Understanding

Roger Scruton (2017: 12–13) writes:

> ... science is not the only way to pursue knowledge. There is moral knowledge too, which is the province of practical reason; there is emotional knowledge, which is the province of art, literature, and music. And just possibly there is transcendental knowledge, which is the province of religion. Why privilege science, just because it sets out to explain the world? Why not give weight to the disciplines that interpret the world and so help us to be at home in it? ...
>
> Culture is not a science and 'is as much an activity of the rational mind as science'.

Even if science has within itself the ability to explain everything that ever was and ever will be, there will always be other ways of deriving meaning, of interpreting reality, of making sense of the world around us. Science is just part of our world, so we lose a great deal of our understanding of ourselves if we see things entirely from a scientific perspective.

In *Admirable Evasions: How Psychology Undermines Morality*, the psychiatrist and writer Theodore Dalrymple sums up the human predicament. He points out it can never be wholly explained from an objective, scientific perspective:

> ... the inherent tragic dimension of human existence [is] a dimension that only literature (and other forms of art), but not psychology, can capture. ... Without an appreciation of the tragic dimension, all is shallowness; and those without it are destined for a life that is nasty and brutish, if not necessarily short. (Dalrymple, 2015: 118–119)

By ignoring the human, subjective sphere in which education takes place, education itself is deadened. In the 1920s, the Vienna Circle attempted to introduce the verifiability principle – a reductive approach to make all knowledge observably and logically true. Metaphysics, aesthetics, ethics and religion all had to be stated in verifiable scientific language or be declared nonsense. It is this same objectifying approach that attempts to make education data-driven and objective – responsive only to input–output techniques of knowledge transfer and measured to within an inch of itself. Under its reductionist lens, education ceases to be anything remarkable. It becomes an impersonal transaction in which the amount of demonstrable knowledge is valued over the quality. The qualitative nature of knowledge is difficult to grade fairly, which means that it is devalued when compared to the knowledge that can satisfy examination criteria. The curriculum needs to cover a range of different ways of knowing, some of which might be extremely difficult to assess or grade in ways that machine schools demand. This is most obviously the case in the arts.

Ways of Knowing

Adam Zeman, a professor of cognitive and behavioural neurology at the University of Exeter Medical School, writes in *A Portrait of the Brain* (2009: 198): 'Art is particular, personal, specific – even if of universal relevance – science strives to be general, impersonal, abstract. Each has much to say about experience: the approaches are complementary. Both offer keys to the kingdom, helping us to understand our minds and lives.' Curriculum must cover not only a range of different ways of knowing the world, but must also open up these areas to scrutiny via conversation and the making of new ways of seeing – for example, reading poetry, discussing it and writing it. If we are aiming for a broad and rich curriculum that enables young children to make sense of their lives and think about how they might live, then we must ensure that the curriculum is true to different ways of seeing the world, rather than just focusing on those that are transactional or instrumental.

All the subjects we offer in a curriculum have an equal relevance to the pursuit of wisdom, beauty and truth. Children should be educated in a way that respects these different lenses and their traditions. They should be free to make their own lives.

Free Will

> The contemporary scientific image of human behavior is one of neurons firing, causing other neurons to fire, causing our thoughts and deeds, in an unbroken chain that stretches back to our birth and beyond. In principle, we are therefore completely predictable.
>
> Stephen Cave, There's No Such Thing as Free Will (2016)

If we believe that children are 100% predictable and that it is possible to achieve 100% accuracy in predicting any pupil's response to any particular stimulus, and if we could guarantee that with certain inputs every child could achieve a certain qualification, so when they venture into the 'real world' they could do a specific job to a predetermined standard, would we have reached the ultimate goal of education? Conversely, if we believe that human beings are unpredictable and that we have free will, then the job of the teacher is to teach the pupil so they might live life to the full, free to create their own adventures as well as to recognise their common cause and humanity. It strikes me that whether or not we believe in free will makes a huge difference to how we approach education.

The scientist Benjamin Libet's (1985) research into neural activity has given added impetus to the possibility that free will is an illusion. He carried out an experiment in which he observed a 'readiness potential': a few hundred milliseconds before a human being is consciously aware that they are about to do something, the brain shows signs of activity. Libet surmises that the consequent muscular reaction is the result of brain activity, rather than the conscious self, willing it into action.

In *Free Will*, Sam Harris (2012: 65) concludes that we don't have free will and sums it up thus: 'Am I free to change my mind? Of course not. It can only change me,' echoing Libet's conclusions about the readiness potential. The question is problematic: is he somewhere *beyond* his mind? In other words, *I* can change *me*; my mind is not separate from me. It is something true to my own sense of self, so to dismiss it as a purveyor of illusory free will is surely absurd.

The determinist voices do not go away, even if we try to ignore them. There is still the uncomfortable notion that we are driven by unconscious processes, but no one knows whether the readiness potential is any such thing. It is possible that what Libet observed was a result of the brain laying out options for the participants to consider consciously, which might be necessary to enable a subsequent decision. It might be like warming the engine before we apply pressure to the accelerator and place our hands on the steering wheel. The speed and direction of travel is then up to us.

It is worth bearing in mind that the nature of Libet's experiment, which took place under laboratory conditions, was observing participants who were deciding whether to flex a finger. The study didn't measure their reasoning about whether or not to take part in the experiment, something which might have involved more deliberation than simply raising a finger. Nor did it measure the participants' understanding when the experiment was described to them, when they might have been considering whether to do it or not.

If Harris (2012: 64) is correct in asserting that free will is illusory, that 'thoughts simply arise in our mind' and that the brain reacts in potentially predictable ways in each individual, then how we go about educating children should be more akin to reprogramming. Harris understands why the idea that free will is illusory might be unpalatable. He thinks we might worry that we will become dehumanised as we reach further scientific understandings about ourselves. He is damn right! If we have no free will and are biological machines, then of course we are dehumanised. It's true: free will is one of the things that make us feel most human. If it is mere illusion then we will have to live with that fact. Although we could probably live in a pretty similar way, the fact that, essentially, we would all be zombies would surely see our strongly held beliefs in our freedom erode over time as whatever happened to us in our lifetimes would no longer be our responsibility.

'Well,' said Pooh … 'Do Tiggers like honey?'

'They like everything,' said Tigger cheerfully …

Tigger took a large mouthful of honey … and then he said in a very decided voice: 'Tiggers don't like honey.'

'Oh!' said Pooh … 'I thought they liked everything.' (Milne, 1956 [1928]: 23–26)

Tigger thinks he likes everything, but when he tastes honey he knows immediately that he doesn't like it. Are we all like Tigger – devoid of anything except instant opinions? Are we unable to acquire the capacity to educate our palates?

If the preferences of the pupil who hates Shakespeare and loves Marvel Comics are hardwired into their brain, what should the English teacher do? If we can't help what we like or dislike, are teachers left with no option but to allow pupils to follow their thoughts and desires wherever they might lead? It could be argued that it would be cruel not to. In fact, the pupil *can* work on changing their mind about Shakespeare and I, as their teacher, will be the one to help them do it – because I want them to love Shakespeare. This is when their thoughts and consciousness become so important: when their will comes into contact with the will of another. Pupil and teacher are involved in a free dialogue through which they can change their views, freely, and, at the very least, empathise with another's point of view.

Kevin Mitchell, the aforementioned associate professor of genetics and neuroscience, thinks that we do make choices, though these choices are constrained. He suggests that the brain learns from choices we have made in the past to predict possible futures, and, in turn, to inform decisions. He suggests that this is 'free will in action'. However, as we do not have to make major decisions for much of the time, we can rely on: habits, how we have learned to act over time, behaviours informed by our subconscious and our genetic inheritance. Mitchell asks whether we can choose to act in a particular way despite having opposing tendencies. He believes that we can:

> This may be effortful – it may require habits of introspection and a high degree of self-awareness and discipline – but it can clearly be done. In fact, one of the strongest pieces of evidence that we really do have free will is that some people seem to have more of it than others. (Mitchell, 2018a)

How we teach and what we teach is one way of helping pupils to acquire 'habits of introspection and a high degree of self-awareness and discipline', to realise how they can use their will to make choices and changes in the world. It is education's gift to furnish pupils with the ability to think about those choices, and to know when they ought to intervene and when it's OK to go with the flow.

The choices we make are, of course, tied to our feelings: the will is not a matter for the logical mind alone. And neither is education. A curriculum cannot be said to be knowledge-rich if it doesn't help children to know, respond to and learn about their emotional selves, as well as learn to use their emotions and their will constructively to broaden and deepen their experience of life.

Feelings

Where is the truth in our subjective view? What we call love is vital to us as humans. When a relationship falls apart we can be hurt beyond compare. There might be objective explanations for our heartbreak, but those explanations may offer little comfort or consolation. The truth that speaks to us at that moment might be in our rage or sorrow, or possibly found in a song or poem.

Similarly, when a loved one dies, we might know about the science of grief but also we know that it's not enough. We look for human sympathy, consoling music or a poem by our favourite author. We search for subjective descriptions and empathetic feelings. When we are at our most raw we need the comforts of love and art; famously, 'Musick has Charms to sooth a savage Breast' (Congreve, 1697: I, i). The great works of culture enable us to understand ourselves as human beings and give us a way of coping with all that life might throw at us. Yes, we are at the bidding of our natural selves and our culture, but within that our understanding is emotional and communicated in primal ways – through touch, language, music, art. Such choices can be taught and honed and, yes, improved. We can learn to love certain things and see why they might be good for us.

This is a major reason why the quality, depth and breadth of the curriculum is such an essential part of good schooling. It is not just the quantity of reading that is important, despite the millions of words that apparently make up the 'word gap' between children from high, middle and low socioeconomic backgrounds (see Hart and Risley, 1995). It is the quality of the reading that makes a real difference to people's lives. We need to be free to feel and to articulate our feelings in a way that enables us to embrace our emotional selves and the human condition artfully. This freedom comes from learning about how to be-in-the-world.

Instead of seeing the input–output of knowledge as a straight trajectory of cause and effect, individual pupils must experience a range of emotions in their learning. It is important to recognise that, ultimately, they are free to feel, to agree or not agree. If all goes well, they will develop an aesthetic awareness and will be enabled to bring words to bear that will uncover, develop and create their innermost thoughts and feelings. Pupils need language to experience their richest emotional selves, to respond expansively to art and culture, and to express what it is to be them.

The curriculum that attends to the broad range of human expression in a variety of ways, especially beyond the mark scheme, is one that can help to give meaning to the whole child. In the short term, it might mean encouraging them not to rush to judgement. Good judgements require the development of a critical eye. How we teach children can help them to develop this discernment. A wise curriculum is set up in such a way as to maximise the ability to cast a critical eye on crucial areas of human life and art. And to do this we need to think about the entire school experience. The whole child is not wholly educated unless we attend to the whole environment. If we want wiser pupils, we need to provide wiser, broader and richer environments in which they can flourish.

Chapter 10

Knowledge and Understanding

We shall not cease from exploration

And the end of all our exploring

Will be to arrive where we started

And know the place for the first time.

T. S. Eliot, 'Little Gidding', *Four Quartets* (1943)

If we want our curriculum to be knowledge-rich, we also need it to be, on occasion, understanding-rich too. What is the difference between knowledge and understanding? There seems to be a qualitative difference, but what might that be? 'I know – I mean, I *really* know,' is often said to emphasise the difference. Like being in love – I mean, *really* in love – knowing something well sometimes needs an intensifier. Yet, in knowing something well, we can sometimes have an impression of breakthrough, of seeing something afresh, as if for the first time.

Eliot's 'Little Gidding' gives us an insight into how we might differentiate knowledge and understanding. We can think we know something really well, but there is a step beyond this when it becomes part of our being, our values, the way we see the world. This qualitative difference can be summed up as 'arriving back where we started and knowing it for the first time'. This moves us from knowing something almost impersonally to having a personal stake in our understanding of it. According to the *Chambers Dictionary of Etymology*, in Old English 'understanding' meant 'to stand in the midst of'. It is this intimate involvement that is important; instead of merely knowing something, we have absorbed it into our way of making meaning of the world. It has helped us to reaffirm or revise our values. Understanding occurs when something becomes part of our narrative. More than just fitting into a schema, this narrative is one that is core to us: 'I have made this part of my thinking' means, 'I base my actions on this presupposition about how the world works.'

An understanding person is qualitatively different to a knowledgeable person. Understanding in this sense suggests human sympathy. Understanding is qualitatively different to knowing. For me, it was becoming a parent that made this difference clear. A child suffering has always evoked my sympathy, but since becoming a father I find that when I hear of a child suffering or of a parent experiencing loss, I am beside myself. I empathise. I feel it in a visceral way because I have experienced something similar myself. Now that I can imagine something awful happening to my own child, I can say that I understand it as if for the first time.

Hans-Georg Gadamer (1989 [1975]: 322) wrote: 'Understanding … is a special case of applying something universal to a particular situation'. To know something is one thing, but to apply that knowledge and to make personal sense of it is to truly understand it: 'understanding always involves something like applying the text to be understood to the interpreter's present situation' (ibid.: 318–319). This personal sense of knowing suggests that a teacher sometimes has a different purpose than simply being a provider of knowledge. If we want to impart wisdom, and encourage our pupils to pursue wisdom, then knowing alone is not enough. Understanding also has a role to play. When teaching something new, we might need to suggest that understanding this fully will take time, maybe even a lifetime. This is one reason why we need to object to pursuing a list of 'learning objectives' in each lesson.

Teachers need to elicit empathy and personal involvement with the knowledge that is being taught. Not with all of it, by any means, but some parts of schooling should be designed to stimulate an awakening of the pupils' inner worlds and thus prompt them to express the thoughts, emotions and passions which lie within. The stories we tell, the values we espouse and the perspectives we explain – and how they conflict and change over time – is how we help our pupils to find their moorings or even set sail on stormy seas.

The Inner World

The task of the modern educator is not to cut down jungles but to irrigate deserts ... By starving the sensibility of our pupils we only make them easier prey to the propagandist when he comes.

C. S. Lewis, *The Abolition of Man* (1943)

If we were to accept a purely materialist view of schooling, then knowing would be explained as an outcome of neural activity. Teaching and learning could bypass the need to involve the child in any way, apart from telling them that this injection of knowledge might cause a slight spasm.

We talk of colour, for example, and yet we know that colour does not exist in the 'real world' – it is a construct of the brain and the body in commune with the world. Through learning we reach an understanding of certain sensations that enable us to share this knowledge about redness so that others can understand it too. Therefore, we should address ourselves to the sensibilities of our pupils. It is the subjective, inner world that is real to our human experience of ourselves – albeit a tragic world of suffering and pain, ignorance and misunderstanding, doubt and uncertainty, as well as celebration, joy and love.

But the inner world on its own is not enough either. We need to link it with the world around us to develop a deep understanding of ourselves, our community and beyond. In order to give these aspects of our lives richness and fulfilment, we have poetry, music, art and dance. This inner life is a place that we nurture and cultivate through our interactions with the world and with each other. It is the teacher's responsibility to know how best to impart this knowledge and how to engender human involvement and understanding.

In his treatise, *De Magistro* (On the Teacher), St Augustine suggests that to teach a human being there are three parties in the relationship: the two who wish to communicate (teacher and pupil) and the third, God. To *know* something we have to know it by heart – we have to love it. This inner heart is shared by us all; it is the place where we acknowledge our human frailties, the tragedy of man. For Augustine, the inner truth reveals itself to us 'through a glass darkly' and cannot be reached except through the one true teacher, the universal God who is within us all. His is a spiritual understanding, where the universal becomes personal and where sympathy meets knowledge. It is where all things ultimately make sense to us, not just individually but in the realisation that this personal view links us to the whole of humanity. The inner world is conversational for Augustine: for him, it is a conversation with God. For others, it might be the sense that our deepest struggles may not even have words, just a sense or a feeling. It is this that unites us as humankind. As Michael Polanyi (1966: 4) puts it: 'We know more than we can tell.'

St Augustine's 'Steps to Wisdom', in Book II of *De Doctrina Christiana* (On Christian Doctrine), are fear, piety, knowledge, resolution, counsel, purification of heart (understanding) and wisdom. An education in the pursuit of wisdom recognises the tragedy of the human condition. For Larry Siedentop, in his book *Inventing the Individual* (2015), Augustine embedded the idea of the will as a halfway point between reason and appetite. Where we have the freedom to choose between good and evil, to choose good we need to have 'a will by which we seek to live a good and upright life and to attain unto perfect wisdom'.

The Augustinian self is made up of both autonomy and dependency. He recognises the importance of the emotional life and knowing ourselves, but with a humble awareness of our flaws. True wisdom is the coming together of the intellectual life with the emotional, the cultural and the physical: 'Augustine becomes the incomparable champion of human frailty, of the dependence of the upright will on divine support. That, in turn, makes Augustine an obstinate opponent of anything like a perfectionist ethic' (Siedentop, 2015: 105–106). Augustine was sceptical of the desire for pure rationalism: the mind could not tell love what to do and humankind could not be perfect. Non-theoretical understanding has to have a place – a place that is very difficult to describe theoretically.

In our secular age, where God is dead and art has become entertainment and commerce, our commonality has been reduced. It has been stripped of both spirituality and sensibility. Many of us, myself included, can't contemplate bringing God back in; we just don't believe that He exists. But without some sense of the spiritual there can be self-absorption and self-obsession. We medicate the resulting lack of well-being with drugs and self-help books and the platitudes of well-meaning but fatuous commentators. The chasm of meaning in our lives is clearly not satisfied by knowledge alone. We need understanding and a way of engaging with the world that is not purely theoretical or measurable.

The best replacement for a dead God is an ersatz one. We need meaning, and Athena gives us the opportunity to bring back truth and other ways of experiencing meaning. For us to value wisdom, we need to worship at the altar of Athena. By positing Athena against the Machine, we set up the idea that, beyond the grade, children need help to find meaning in their lives: they need help to prize our myths as truthful representations of the ways we might live and the values that we might live by. Knowledge is joined by experience and judgement; education is a sagacious enterprise.

There is a mechanistic view of education which posits that learning is what is retained in the brain. It is a completely internalised model, one which is also driven by genes. There is also another mechanistic view which asserts that what shapes our thought is completely externalised, that it is social factors which play a large part in how we see and are seen in the world. Both views devalue the role of the individual human in shaping their world. Despite the constraints placed on us by genetics and environment, it is where our inner and outer worlds converge that we can find ourselves most human and most free to shape our world.

… innerworldliness is based on the phenomenon of *world*, which in turn belongs to the fundamental constitution of Dasein as an essential structural factor of being-in-the-world.

Martin Heidegger, *Being and Time* (1953)

Education in the pursuit of wisdom is rooted in human subjectivity – how the inner and outer world connect. Connecting the two together is the mind, which can be thought of as the mechanism through which the brain extends into the world and the world extends into the brain. It recognises the human being as a creature within the world and the locus through which the world is understood.

At this moment you are reading this book and contemplating it. The book and its contents are external – the words have been worked over by me and now they are being thought about by you. Your thoughts are internal: you are simultaneously looking at the book and it is having an impact on you. However, the book's externality is at once internal and external. Your thoughts are seemingly able to transcend your skull: as you read the words they appear to be both inside and outside of you at the same time. Your subjective view is vital, but you would not have the view if you hadn't read this book. In addition, the object (book) and its subjective thoughts (contents) are being thought about by you in a different way to others reading the same content. In *Innate: How the Wiring of Our Brains Shapes Who We Are*, Kevin Mitchell describes the role of genetics in this, and asks whether we all see the world in the same way. He answers with an emphatic no: 'these differences in perception affect not just what we sense, or how we sense it, but also what meaning different stimuli have for us and, at a very fundamental and deeply subjective level, how we all think about various things in our world' (Mitchell, 2018b: 154).

To deny the subjective human gaze in the educative process denies human being itself. This is not to say that because we all see the world differently, no one has a purchase on truth and everything is relative. There is truth, but finding it can be difficult. The world shapes us and we shape the world – we can't discern things beyond our capacity to know them as they are revealed to us. To help us uncover meaning we need teachers, artists, scientists and others, all of us working together in the community of minds to fashion a form of wisdom and understanding about the world in which the truth can be found.

All pupils need an education which appeals to their reason *and* their emotions, to their understanding of the (as near as can be ascertained) objective view on the world *and* the subjective, to their need to know *and* their need to take part. This is determined by relationships within the classroom, most importantly between the teacher and the child – who, at that moment, is being appreciated not as a data point but as a human being.

Curriculum – A Grand Tour

The curriculum should be the first port of call for any school. Schools have a duty to help pupils articulate their understanding of self, their cultural milieu and the natural world. Pupils need to recognise their commonality with humanity as well their differences. They need to have a well-developed aesthetic, philosophic and scientific sense. They need to develop a palate, their own tastes and an understanding of different perspectives in order to find themselves authentically at home in the world.

What we teach is paramount. The curriculum must be carefully selected in terms of the stories we tell and also what we leave out. In earlier times, in order to make up for the limited education on offer at public schools, upper-class young men from Europe would go on a Grand Tour. This was recognised as 'an ideal means of imparting taste and knowledge and of arousing curiosity in the mind of a youth … who was expected to return from his travels with a broadened mind as well as a good command of foreign languages, a new self-reliance and self-possession as well as a highly developed taste and grace of manner' (Hibbert, 1969: 15).

The Curriculum Grand Tour is not a journey towards a single destination, but an adventure, a catalogue of experiences from the sacred to the profane. All life should be here. There is a need to travel into the unknown and the uncertain, all the while feeling sure that we will return home again and yet know it as if for the first time. Pupils need to be taught about tradition, its wisdom and truths. Pupils need to be helped to articulate how to accept and/or challenge these truths through action, sensibility and reason. Pupils need to learn how to realise their own self – self-actualisation, if you will. Pupils need to know how to find themselves at home in the world and also how to reach out beyond it and express themselves in their various groupings and communities – from family to locale, nation, planet and perhaps even beyond, metaphysically and cosmologically.

It is how to make a spirit of adventure commensurate with the feeling of being at home that is one of the great imponderables of curriculum and education. Will the Grand Tour take us away from where we feel most at home?

Chapter 11

What Is a School For?

Ever since the dawn of civilisation, people have craved for an understanding of the ... world ... But even if we do find a complete theory of everything, it is just a set of rules and equations. What is it that breathes fire into the equations, and makes a universe for them to describe?

Stephen Hawking, Opening Ceremony of the
2012 London Paralympic Games

Athena establishes our schools as places where the central concern is the pursuit of wisdom. Wisdom is about the ability to make good judgements, to discern and discriminate based on values which are considered and examined throughout a lifetime. It has a necessary relationship to truth and knowledge. However, wisdom is a slippery concept. It lacks precision, and consequently it lacks the rigour of something objectively measurable. Like searching for the pot of gold at the end of the rainbow, humankind can never achieve full wisdom, and therefore the institution which has to deliver it has a problematic target in the yearly review of results. Where does the pursuit of wisdom fit in with the concerns of contemporary schooling and the need to collect data on everything that can be pinned down?

If grades could be a proxy for wisdom then this might not be so bad, but the obsession with the pursuit of grades above all else has the unintended consequence of reducing the likelihood of the individual and the institution gaining much wisdom at all. Other notions of truth have been sidelined in the pursuit of cherry-picked measurable ends.

Pupils are studying certain disciplines for their transactional value rather than their intrinsic truth. 'What subjects will get pupil X to university?' and

'What university and course will deliver the highest earnings over the years to come?' have become more important than studying what you love or are passionate about. This is especially true if you are a paying customer who will end up thousands of pounds in debt.

It is impossible to track the progress of a pupil's understanding of wisdom. Consequently, it tends to get replaced by measurements that purport to represent it – or, at least, come as near as we can get to measuring the instrumental success of education: how much a child can remember, how socially mobile they are, how they are performing compared to others in their cohort and subcategory, whether they are outperforming their peers at the intersection. Indicators are developed that are intended to denote pupils' well-being and how smart they are – from IQ and EQ, to CATs and SATs, to character and personality types. Some even purport to show their 'learning style' and dominant brain hemisphere. These traits are identified and measured and are absorbed into the Machine as 'facts'. No matter that some of these measures are controversial and extremely dubious; the controversy is cloaked by respectable-looking pseudo-assessment tools.

The psychologist James Flynn (of Flynn effect fame) believes that we should go a step further than suggesting that any gain in IQ is a gain in intelligence. He proposes that we break down intelligence into the following factors: 'solving mathematical problems, interpreting the great works of literature, finding on-the-spot solutions, assimilating the scientific worldview, critical acumen, and wisdom' (Flynn, 2009: 10). If schooling is to achieve anything, it should help children to do these things, but it is hard to pin down what intelligence might be, let alone wisdom. Flynn suggests that wisdom exists 'When human beings integrate the intellectual and moral virtues into a functional whole … one cannot know the good without loving the good. It would be like saying one knew what made a great painting beautiful without having any appreciation of its beauty' (ibid.: 159). He discusses the role of Aristotelian practical wisdom – that knowing about something is allied to its practice and performance. He advances the need for intellectual and moral virtues, sympathetic empathy and the human dynamic, which includes the cognitive skills around which no measure yet exists (although this does not preclude their importance). His conclusion is that wisdom resides where our individuality and our similarity meet, where the objective and the subjective come together. Where knowledge meets values and where knowing becomes understanding.

Flynn believes that wisdom will go unnoticed if it is not measured, so he wants to devise measures for wisdom – which he considers to be more important than IQ. He proposes a formal test for wisdom: 'The aim of WICA theory would be to measure wisdom, intelligence, and critical acumen on the levels of social trends and individual differences' (ibid.: 161). As much as I agree with his aims, his desire for measurement is the essence of my problem with the machine worldview. Bureaucrats deal with uncertainty by giving traits a measure (or proxies to measure) in the hope that this will force schools to pay attention to wisdom, character and the like. However, this has the unintended consequence of neglecting areas that are essential to the pursuit of wisdom – that which we do not know. There are good reasons why the arts, philosophy and other forms of scholarship deal with a world of uncertainty. We understand this world tentatively, getting only glimpses of the transcendent and the unknown.

If measurement, allied with ersatz objectivity, takes the place of the pursuit of something so nebulous as the art of being wise, then what foolishness will we unleash? Proxies for wisdom will take the place of the actual pursuit of wisdom.

Art

Petyr Baelish: Knowledge is power. ...

Cersei Lannister: Power is power.

Game of Thrones (season 2, episode 1: 'The North Remembers')

And bliss is bliss. In these days of 24/7 information we are in danger of knowledge overload. Anyone can access knowledge, but whether they understand it is another matter. Far from being 'power', a surfeit of knowledge might even be a weakness: a lot of knowledge leaves us powerless to understand or act. In a world of excessive information what is needed is the ability to discriminate; being able to sort the wheat from the chaff has never been more important. This is why teachers are essential. Their job is to help pupils form narratives and schemas through which they can make sense of the knowledge to which they are exposed. As teachers, we must help pupils to become wiser. The need for peace, quiet and contemplation is also vital; moments without more stuff to learn, just time with what is. The pursuit of wisdom is a long-term project in which we come to terms with our ignorance as well as our understanding.

The pursuit of wisdom is magnificent in that it envelops all of time. There is no end in sight for science, art or the humanities. There is too much to know and more is being added all the time. We cannot put a full stop on knowledge. It has no completion date. An exam is an important hiatus along the way; it is not the end. The pause must neither become the end nor replace the pursuit. This is why understanding narratives and perspectives is essential: to contextualise, to sort and to try to come to terms with new knowledge as it comes into our orbit. A school with Athena at its heart serves all time, not just finite exam time. Because it cares for its pupils, dammit. It cares for humanity and the common pursuit. This demands a cultural dexterity and the ability to not fall apart in the face of the shock of the new.

In a mechanical education, culture is seen as capital rather than as something with intrinsic worth. Watching a performance of *Tristan und Isolde* should be about transcendence, not what we can trade in for social mobility. No wonder the Machine struggles with art, preferring the term 'creativity' as a marketable concept and 'creative industries' as a career path rather than an oxymoron. Art gives us a way to appreciate beauty.

Beauty

Beauty is truth, truth beauty – that is all

Ye know on earth, and all ye need to know.

Keats, 'Ode on a Grecian Urn' (1820)

[We] will have to surrender before ... the absolute and unstoppable polytheism of Beauty.

Umberto Eco, *On Beauty: A History of a Western Idea* (2004)

If we want to see how the machine approach affects education, then examining what has happened to the 'aesthetic' subjects can be eye-opening.

What of beauty? According to the assessment criteria for the Edexcel international GCSE in art and design, a pupil is expected to have 'critical understanding', 'take risks' and have an awareness of roles and work practices in the 'creative and cultural industries'. The aesthetics of fine art are allied to 'intellectual' and 'conceptual' ideas, not what makes fine art fine. The mark scheme reflects the pupil's ability to understand 'visual language', 'explore ideas' and 'refine work' (Edexcel, 2017).

The mechanical approach can't tackle the subjective – it daren't even go there. We no longer have a language for, or understanding of, beauty. We are frightened to even broach the idea of beauty as truth. What a pupil needs to do to achieve a top grade in art and design can be communicated, seemingly, in objective terms. That this is subjectivity dressed up as objectivity seems not to be a concern.

Where does this leave our pupils? They are left thinking that there is only one truth – the way to pass exams – and beyond that there is only relativism, with beauty reduced to the more mundane 'visual language'. With so much riding on the final grade, they are desperate to be taught only those things that will appear in the exam. The rest is 'whatever'. Unfortunately, some schools succumb to the pressure to provide the exam delivery mechanism ad infinitum.

Trying to articulate the not-yet-understood is the precipice along which art walks. Risk-taking in an art exam shouldn't be something safely factored into the mark scheme; instead it should be the angst-ridden potential for abject failure in every exam entry. Just because beauty is understood subjectively, it does not mean that everything is beautiful. Perhaps this is where art can fail – when it crosses the unwritten boundaries of taste, judgement and sensibility. We can detect the difference. An education for wisdom must help young people across this difficult terrain by giving them a rich and in-depth aesthetic education.

Truth

The only alternative to incorporating notions of truth and falsehood into an account of education will involve … the assumption that legitimate, educational, forms of persuasion can be distinguished from others simply by their methods: for instance, they are supposed to be specially rational, or to be uniquely directed to the interests of those being persuaded, where neither rationality nor the pupils' interests are understood in terms of a concern for truth.

Bernard Williams, *Truth and Truthfulness:*
An Essay in Genealogy (2002)

Schools are either about the pursuit of wisdom and a concern for truth, or they are about nothing. The free exchange of knowledge and ideas, and discussions around values and meaning between teachers and pupils, is the purest form of education. This involves different teachers using different viewpoints to uncover different perspectives on wisdom. This is the stuff that informs the narratives that children learn. The classroom must be liberated from the Machine. The secret to a great education is to trust in teachers and enable them to follow the tradition of scholarship in the quest for wisdom. However, teachers must work collaboratively; curriculum design is not a singular pursuit.

Power

Today's identity politics ... teaches students to think in a way antithetical to what a liberal arts education should do. When I was at Yale in the 1980s, I was given many tools for understanding the world. By the time I graduated, I could think about things as a utilitarian or a Kantian, as a Freudian or a behaviourist, as a computer scientist or a humanist. I was given many lenses to apply to any one situation. But nowadays, students who major in departments that prioritize social justice over the disinterested pursuit of truth are given just one lens – power – and told to apply it to all situations. Everything is about power. This is not an education.

Jonathan Haidt, Wriston Lecture: The Age of Outrage: What It's Doing to Our Universities, and Our Country, Manhattan Institute (2017)

The free exchange between teachers and pupils must not be maligned by the underlying assumption that relationships are always about power; that the entire curriculum is an act of subjugation; that each individual work, idea or artefact studied is potentially a result of imperialist dogma or an act of oppression of the great unwashed by the bourgeoisie. This approach replaces teacher and pupil – and the artists, writers and thinkers and their works – with something beyond their control, the identity that is deemed by their social selves. If we are all slaves to the external forces of capital and power, then there is no beauty or truth outside that of a transaction between unequal forces. This pseudo-social-scientific approach dehumanises: it sees us not as potentially free but as permanent victims of societal ills, forever reactive to unseen forces of oppression.

A good education doesn't offer just one lens through which to see ourselves and the world; it offers a wide variety of lenses. Whatever reductive pressures are exerted on the curriculum or the teaching of a subject, those of us who have an interest in what we broadly term 'the liberal arts' need to ensure that we teach and design courses which offer up arguments rather than simply presenting narrow answers or a specific worldview. The pursuit of wisdom is never served by insisting that one way of seeing the world has dominion over all others.

Conversation brings individual minds together. It is only by engaging in debate, by testing out ideas and hypotheses, that we can free up individuals to think for themselves, and thus enable them to add to the great conversation in a way that opens and engages minds rather than closes and disengages. A relativist can leave all others numb by saying, 'Truth is an individual construct, so leave me alone.' Cultural relativism is antithetical to a liberal arts education.

Educational institutions should not be places which purport to know the one true way to truth. This awareness should give us great hope in that it elevates the importance of the voices of those who teach different subjects, the voices of those they teach about, the voices of those who are taught and the voices of those who will follow on. Edmund Burke's (1899 [1790]) social contract between the dead, the living and the yet-to-be-born reminds us of the importance of not just thinking of ourselves and our contemporaries as those with particular insight, but that by coming together we might find ourselves closer to wisdom. Midgley (2005: 356) describes human life as an 'ill-lit aquarium': we can never see the whole and instead peer in through a variety of small windows. Each viewpoint has a truth but it can't enable us to experience what the whole truth might be.

Perspectivism

There is only a perspectival seeing, only a perspectival 'knowing'; and the more affects we allow to speak about a matter, the more eyes, different eyes, we know how to bring to bear on one and the same matter, that much more complete will our 'concept' of this matter, our 'objectivity' be.

Friedrich Nietzsche, *On the Genealogy of Morality* (1887)

The curriculum needs to offer ways of seeing and making sense of the world. A good curriculum is not merely focused on knowledge but on how that knowledge is organised into narratives. These narratives, in turn, are organised by competing values and offer differing perspectives on our understandings of the world. The more viewpoints we can offer, the more likely we are to educate successfully. These perspectives need to offer breadth and they should also be experienced in depth. Although this means that inevitable compromises will need to be made, young people should experience learning through as many broad lenses as we can muster – traditionally, the arts, sciences, languages, humanities, physical and metaphysical studies.

If we narrow or reduce our perspectives, we are more likely to falter than we are to glimpse the truth. Pupils need to access a full and varied curriculum from an early age, and for as long as possible, so their thinking and experiencing does not atrophy over time. Subjects should be taught with dialogue, argument and debate at their heart, to ensure that different viewpoints can clash nicely throughout the heart of the school's offer. Pupils should also get a good grounding in philosophy, ethics and aesthetics.

In order to ensure a good range of perspectives, there needs to be a good range of subjects on offer in schools. This means starting specialist subject teaching sometime during primary education, expanding the offer during Key Stage 3 and ensuring that pupils are able to access a wide range of subjects at Key Stage 4. The arts, humanities, languages, social sciences, technology and physical/health education options should be kept up for as long as possible, alongside English, maths and the 'hard' sciences.

Measures that reduce breadth in the name of an instrumental purpose (such as the English Baccalaureate) or categorise certain subjects as 'facilitating' others should be treated critically. Is it wise for a child to have their perspectives on the world narrowed in this way and at such a critical time? A levels themselves can constitute a drastic reduction in outlook at an important time of intellectual and cultural engagement in the world.

Can schools do more to alleviate this? There are opportunities through the International Baccalaureate and the home-grown initiatives that schools are instituting themselves, as well as a rich academic and cultural co-curricular offer (without the necessity for formal grading) to ensure that pupils keep being curious about the world.

A good extra- (or co-)curricular programme is essential, including the traditional school productions, orchestras, exhibitions, sports teams, debating teams and so on. Involvement in voluntary work and events that entail community outreach are another great opportunity. A house system can help to develop leadership skills and widen participation in team events beyond the elite inter-school level. Even for those pupils who intend to study more vocational subjects, there should be occasions for academic/cultural study and extracurricular activities. All work and no play/reading/writing/thinking about the big questions makes Jack and Jill dull. An expansive curriculum gives young people the chance to flourish.

Chapter 12

Educating for Freedom

To be free is nothing; to become free is very heaven.

Attributed to Johann Gottlieb Fichte

Gentlemen, there are questions that worry me; solve them for me. You for example want human beings to give up their old habits and adjust their will so that it accords with the requirements of science and common sense. But how do you know that human beings not only can but *must* be transformed in this way?

Fyodor Dostoevsky, Notes from Underground (1864)

In *The Case Against Education* (2018), the economist Bryan Caplan makes an interesting case for utilitarian education. He argues against a liberal arts education and, in particular, the idea that we should teach 'high culture'. For Caplan, an enlightened 'transformative' education is wasted on the young. He proposes that a liberal arts education should be accessed through the internet by people when (and, crucially, if) they are ready so to do – perhaps when they are older and wiser. Although he believes that this type of education is good for the soul, he judges that, given the choice, most people wouldn't bother to sign up for it.

Caplan suggests that good-for-the-soul education belongs to the economic category of a 'merit good' – something that has value beyond that which people would be willing to pay. In order to qualify as a merit good, he proposes that education should have three ingredients: 'worthy content', 'skillful pedagogy' and be taught to 'eager students'. This is difficult to achieve because most teachers are 'boring', the pupils are 'worse' and the content being taught is 'mixed at best' (Caplan, 2018: 240–241). He goes on to state: 'If education is a merit good, then the Internet is a Merit

Machine' and that 'This Merit Machine is swiftly making traditional humanist education policy obsolete' (ibid.: 242).

Caplan proposes that formal education does not open the world of ideas and culture to those who are interested, but rather it forces them onto a great number of uninterested people. He does not see vast swathes of eager pupils desperate to learn about civilisation's greatest treasures; mandating that they must be exposed to certain ideas and cultural products makes them even less keen. He points out that even when all this enlightenment is available for free on the internet, very few people choose to access it. He cites education's unconvincing attempts to open up high culture for the vast majority of people who go through the doors of our schools as a sign of its failure. He believes this is due to the additional mental effort it takes for us to appreciate high culture: the vast majority of people resent the extra thinking involved and thus resort to instant gratification from more accessible types of culture. For Caplan, humanist education doesn't succeed in its major aims, so he proposes that a vocational and technical education should take its place.

Caplan points out that schools turn to other methods to alleviate these problems, but although 'regimentation might be a good way to mould external behaviour' (ibid.: 260), it has no chance of engaging children's hearts and minds. He cites historian of education David Labaree, who suggests that pupils are little more than 'classroom conscripts' who survive by gaming the system and, for the more savvy, feigning a wide range of cultural interests and experiences in order to beef up their personal statement for university entry or to make them look a cut above on their CV. Just don't expect them to talk in any depth at interview about the novels, symphonies, artworks and museums they have mentioned. Crib sheets are enough for the cynical pupil who knows how to play this game.

Good for the Soul

If only schools were determined to teach worthy, difficult content in a skilful way, then we might have more eager pupils. If we actually got them involved in the conversation, rather than seeing their studies as a means to a grade, we might have more pupils who value high culture. Schools have become very utilitarian in their aims – they have already moved too far towards Caplan's view of what an education should be. It is this 'training' in the use of knowledge as transactional or cultural literacy, as opposed to an intrinsic good in itself, which has resulted in cynical pupils, cynical teachers and a view of education as an instrumental device in the material world. Rather than education being good for being, schools are investing in concepts such as cultural capital, social mobility and growth mindset, which have resulted in a devaluation of the things being studied. Why on earth should a child have to study Shakespeare or listen to Beethoven in order to become a lawyer, salesperson or doctor? Why study history in order to design an app or work on the tills at Walmart? No wonder they aren't eager.

Caplan is right to point out that as employers demand higher and higher qualifications, young people rarely use their new-found knowledge in the workplace: 'As long as academic success leads to career success, neither parents nor pupils have much motive to critique the curriculum. How do educators decide which irrelevant subjects to emphasise? ... Students spend over a decade learning piles of dull content they won't use after graduation' (Caplan, 2018: 288). Instead, he thinks that subsidies should be taken away from schools and young people should move out from home sooner and start to pay their own way in society.

In *Enlightenment Now: The Case for Reason, Science, Humanism, and Progress* (2018), Steven Pinker argues that education has led to large rises in IQ and literacy levels and the broadening of Enlightenment values. For him, a liberal education makes people more enlightened, and so the intrinsic good of education is seen through its effects on the population. Pinker also discusses the Flynn effect, which shows that increases in IQ are cultural: we are not getting more intelligent in terms of g (the measure given to general intelligence, which is mainly affected by our genes) but in 'fluid intelligence', which is fed through more abstract and logical thinking. Pinker (2018: 243) writes: 'An analytical mindset is inculcated by formal schooling, even if a teacher never singles it out in a lesson, as long as the curriculum requires understanding and reasoning rather than rote memorisation.' He suggests that abstract reasoning can have a moral sense, and agrees with Flynn that this sort of education, in which 'The cognitive act of extracting oneself from the particulars of one's life and pondering: "There but for the grace of God go I" or "What would the world be like if everyone did this?" can be a gateway to compassion and ethics' (ibid.: 243).

These metaphysical questions take us firmly into the world of philosophy and the arts. On one side we have Caplan's view that an education which embraces high culture is wasted on the great unwashed, and on the other is Pinker's suggestion that it is precisely the type of education that moves beyond the mundane which results in more informed human beings with higher IQs. Unusually, I find myself siding with Pinker. The net effect of our education system becoming more utilitarian and more mechanical might satisfy the desires of our pupils, but in the long run it will do them and society no good whatsoever.

Flynn (2009) argues that, since the 1900s, IQ has been increasing in certain parts of the world due to the cumulative effects set in motion by the Industrial Revolution and cultural shifts, particularly after the Second World War, which have driven the need for people to put on 'scientific spectacles'. This change is not simply due to mass schooling; the wider aspects of our culture also influence how individuals deal with the world. Flynn suggests that it is not improved brain capacity which has boosted the rise in IQ but, by looking at the types of cognitive change that have occurred, that it is down to modernity's more abstract intellectual environment and associated cultural factors.

That some developed nations now see IQ levels stalling might be a sign of the next stage of modernity – for Flynn, affluence – which is dumbing down how we relate to the world. By preparing kids for the job market, teaching to the test and getting them to follow flight paths, we are in danger of making them dumber and our societies less enlightened. Pupils who use knowledge for its transactional worth will become the teachers of the future in an education sector in which decisions about what to study will be oriented around what it is easiest to teach efficiently and for the most measurable, material gain.

Understanding Ourselves

When we absorb great literature, we come face to face with ideas, experiences, and emotions that we might never otherwise encounter in our lifetime. When we read history, we encounter people from a different age and learn from their triumphs and traps. When we study physics and biology, we comprehend the mysteries of the universe and human life. And when we listen to great music, we are moved in ways that reason cannot comprehend.

Zakaria, *In Defense of a Liberal Education* (2015)

We are not born free. We are born into a social world – parents, siblings, families, community, schools and other institutions. As we become increasingly aware of the wider culture (and cultures), we try to make sense of ourselves as individuals, as beings who did not exist until recently and will not exist sometime soon. Our fleeting time on this earth is our tragedy, yet it could be argued that this is the most significant feature of our lives. The pursuit of the truth of our existence might be beyond us individually, or even collectively, but that should not be a reason to ignore it. In fact, it should give us pause to redouble our efforts. It is the duty of the school to help us in that adventure.

The truth about what it is to be human must be addressed in our lives. This need not be some esoteric introversion. Yes, it can be tackled through the questions, 'How do and how might *I* live?' but also, 'How do and how might *we* live?' This living is very much in the cultural realm; it is both particular and universal. It is as citizens of somewhere and anywhere that we exist, both at home and as visitors. It is love, hate and everything in-between: 'The world as we live it is not the world as science explains it, any more than the smile of the Mona Lisa is a smear of pigments on a canvas. But this lived world is as real as the Mona Lisa's smile' (Scruton, 2016: 134).

Schools need to educate their pupils in the pursuit of objective and subjective truths, for it is through both that our freedom is to be found. We understand ourselves in ways that are intrinsic to ourselves. Through these truths we can glimpse our higher being as well as our baser instincts, our tragedy as well as our hope and love. To help us to know and understand this world we have art, a transcendent sense of beauty and the sublime. We have love, giving and being loved, and although these things can be explained and known in an objective way, we experience them intensely in our own particular and subjective ways. These ways are most keenly felt in the modern world as reactions against cold rationalism. This book, knowingly, makes a case for the romantic impulse, although I realise that this is not without its problems.

Romanticism

[P]rogressivism in education is just another name for romanticism.

E. D. Hirsch, Jr, *The Knowledge Deficit* (2006)

E. D. Hirsch, Jr dismisses romanticism as a naive movement that pollutes the education of our children. He argues that romanticism results in a 'natural unfolding' approach to teaching and learning, whereby the teacher waits patiently for the child to be ready to read, write and do sums. Hirsch rightly bemoans the anti-intellectualism that often accompanies this romantic approach to education. To these 'romantic' teachers, Gradgrindian facts are less important than real-life learning. Rather than standing on the shoulders of giants, the desire to teach about higher cultural values is interpreted as being all about the dead white hands of dead white men weighing down heavily on the shoulders of our child-sized protégés. Romantic teachers believe that children should not be forced against their better natures to learn things they might be reluctant to learn, and, by the same token, that the things they might not want to learn are irrelevant to their lives. This approach echoes Caplan's view that when faced with the internet Merit Machine, most people seem to be unwilling to even dip into higher culture. This is not the view of romanticism I am arguing for here.

At the heart of romanticism is the desire to take the human being away from a mechanistic, instrumentalist way of life and into a mode of living that enriches what is often referred to as 'the soul'. Just as Athena breathed life into man, it is what we think of as the soul that should be the central concern of schools. But how do we breathe the stuff of life into our pupils, and how do we do this without falling into the rabbit hole of natural unfolding that Hirsch is so right to condemn?

In schools, an attack on the machine approach – and the defence of a subjective education – could easily result in a child-centred approach in which the rampant satisfying of lots of individual childish whims and wills would clearly be problematic. Little Napoleons expressing themselves in every classroom might be a triumph for romanticism but would also be a behaviour management nightmare. That there is a schism between schools that want placid children to absorb and memorise their worthy knowledge-based lessons and schools that want to encourage the critical and creative child to become the author of their own story and take control of the curriculum does not mean that we have to embrace the latter at the expense of the former. Pandering to the caprices of children is not education; it is its opposite. It might de-escalate certain conflicts in the short term, but in the longer term it leaves a child unable to understand anything beyond the immediate gratification of their own appetites. This isn't freedom; it's slavery to selfishness.

How many of us would enthusiastically read the *Epic of Gilgamesh*, listen to *Tristan und Isolde* or watch a Japanese Noh theatre production? Most of us will never be 'ready' for this sort of thing, which is why we have a formal education system – to take us to places we might not ordinarily choose to go. Schools not only need to take the horse to water, they also have to make it drink. Furthermore (in this overstretched equine metaphor), the horse needs to recognise that when it is thirsty, there is a rich well from which it can – and should – drink. Paradoxically, an education for freedom might mean a pupil experiencing limited freedom in a school setting. But just as a parent might hold a child's hand when teaching them to cross the road, good teachers metaphorically hold their pupils' hands as they navigate the numerous adventures that great schooling affords them.

We educate in order to free human beings to make decisions which can be of benefit to themselves and others. We can't dictate what these decisions might be, but we should lead them to the valuable seams of knowledge from which they can mine understanding, as well as providing the time and place to do it. Freedom is not gained lightly. It involves embracing the lessons of romanticism, for it is here that we find many of humankind's best expressions and understandings of itself. The way we give meaning to ourselves is through our mythos. The romanticism at the core of the curriculum is the building of these myths in order to access beauty and truth.

Logos and Mythos

In *The Roots of Romanticism* (1999), Isaiah Berlin suggested that at the heart of romanticism is an attack on knowledge. The Western scholastic tradition that had been reliant on an unbroken belief in knowing was challenged by the theory that every human being begins tabula rasa. A tradition that, since the Greeks, had extolled the virtue of facts, reason and knowing about 'the best that has been thought and said' (Arnold, 2009 [1869]) was threatened by the suggestion that 'authoritative' sources from the past might have little to commend them.

That romanticism is often perceived as a reaction to the Enlightenment sometimes obscures the similarities between the two – for example, both share a belief in the capability of man to create his own world. But the fundamental differences provide us with a challenge. This can be summed up as the worlds of logos and mythos, the known and the felt, the objective and the subjective. We recognise the border between the two but we also know that they feed each other. If we reject romanticism out of turn, due to its seemingly irrational subjectivity, we are in danger of neglecting much of what makes us human.

Berlin (1999: 144) quotes Adam Müller (1922) who said that science on its own can only reproduce a 'lifeless political State'. It is joined in this life-lessness by 'utilitarianism' and 'the use of machinery'. The importance of romanticism, according to Berlin, is that it points us towards the things that classical and/or scientific man has left out – the unconscious dark forces, our inward experiences, our subjectivity, our freedom, our free will and driven will, our authenticity. If we are to educate for freedom, we have to ensure that our education is full of life

In his lovely little book *Seven Brief Lessons on Physics*, Carlo Rovelli describes the porous border between science and myth. For Rovelli (2016: 67), the value of knowledge only becomes clear at this liminal place: 'Myths nour-ish science and science nourishes myth'. In one we are 'inventing stories' and in the other we are 'following traces in order to find something'. We are of both science and myth. Rovelli explains this porousness through his passion for physics: 'Our reality is made up of our societies, of the emotion inspired by music, of the rich intertwined networks of common knowledge which we have constructed together' (ibid.: 74). And this feeds into our freedom: how the laws of nature are interpreted and act within us brings us to how we make decisions, how we see and how we understand our world.

Isaiah Berlin summarises romanticism in the following way: firstly, as a tri-umph of will – the idea that just as artists create artworks, so we, as artists of our lives, triumph in creating the story of our lives. And, secondly, as a resistance to structure. For Berlin, 'romantic human beings' are free to cre-ate themselves and their own structures, and this results in them being free of authority, tradition and truth. This gives rise to a cycle of perpetual self-creation, whereby human beings are self-organising and self-creating/creative.

According to Berlin, the romantic pursuit is never satisfied and the human being is never complete. We are continually moving but never arrive. We are forever active but never a settled self. We are engaged in the perpetual act of self-authoring a book which might never reach a 'happy ever after' because life can only ever give it an awkward episodic structure. Having to create ourselves and find our own structures is alienating because of the lack of contentment, home and belonging. This can be exhilarating but also potentially debilitating for our well-being.

In *The Romantic Manifesto*, Ayn Rand (1971: 991) writes that there are 'two broad categories of art: Romanticism, which recognizes the existence of man's volition – and Naturalism, which denies it'. Either we believe that man is a slave to the biological and environmental machine, or we trust that he possesses the wherewithal to make choices and shape his own life and that of others. That these choices are constrained by biological and environmental limitations does not restrict man, but instead gives him the potential to be creative and heroic.

Take either of these stances and we have a very different idea about how to educate our children. It is difficult to see how there could be a halfway position. In the process of writing our own story, we have to decide whether we are a victim buffeted by events or a hero facing the world down in our adventurous escapades. If volition is central to romanticism, so are morality and values. We have choices, but these choices are shaped by traditions, rules and our natural limitations. Schools can free the child to make choices, create and author their own lives, while also giving them a sense of home and responsibility so their decisions are defined by a sense of duty, and not obsessed by selfishness. It is through the constraints of discipline that creativity can be unleashed. The creative child is not unmoored and battered by the waves of rough and unpredictable seas; rather, they are given a sturdy boat and the ability to set sail with a mixture of curiosity, excitement and fear. This is the job of curriculum.

We need to encourage children to drink from the well of wisdom. This will come from being educated about the great things, for no better reason than this is good – for the child, for their time and for all time. This is why we teach classic literature: what could be better than an education informed by *Les Misérables*, *Moby-Dick* and *To the Lighthouse*?

The Mind

The soul is a useful metaphor, but it belongs to the dualistic idea that the body is just a physical vessel for the 'real self'. Our conscious self is in dialogue with the unconscious, the material, the environmental and the social. What we call 'soul' is also served by the idea of 'mind'; it is something beyond just a mechanical brain and relates to how we make meaning in the world.

For example, the romantic artist might be looking for inspiration from nature, from the sublime or from extreme emotions. He uses this inspiration in a disciplined and thoughtful manner: drawing out meaning from nature, for example, he adds to the mythos with his art. These great artists can make us better human beings or give us solace in ourselves. In the romantic tradition, we are all the authors of our own stories. As such, we can look to other writers for their stories for inspiration to help us evaluate our own values – how we make sense of the world and how we act within it. Our stories are shaped by human will, emotions and reason: rather than merely accepting our fate, we also have the creative resources to change it.

For Berlin (1999: 170), the romantic desire for freedom from structure and the pre-eminence of the creative will resulted in 'liberalism, toleration, decency and the appreciation of the imperfections of life; some degree of rational self-understanding'. The pursuit of wisdom is a multitudinous art:

We ... owe to romanticism the notion that a unified answer to human affairs is likely to be ruinous ... The notion that there are many values, and that they are incompatible; the notion of plurality, of inexhaustibility, of the imperfection of all human answers and arrangements; the notion that no single answer which claims to be perfect and true, whether in art or in life, can in principle be perfect or true – all this we owe to the Romantics. (Berlin, 1999: 169)

According to Berlin (1999: 162), romanticism undermined the idea that 'in matters of value, politics, morals, aesthetics there are such things as objective criteria'. He refused to determine whether this was a positive contribution or not. But from this belief that all is not set in stone comes freedom. This is summed up in the phrases, 'What do you have in mind?' and 'What do you think?' which imply that we are free. Although this freedom is undoubtedly set within the constraining parameters of nature and tradition, we have a certain degree of liberty to think about how we might live, who we might be and how to forge our way in the world.

Curriculum and Freedom

Man is born free; and everywhere he is in chains. One thinks himself the master of others, and still remains a greater slave than they.

Jean-Jacques Rousseau, *The Social Contract* (1762)

O'er the glad waters of the deep blue sea,

Our thoughts as boundless, and our hearts as free.

Lord Byron, 'The Corsair' (1814)

Rousseau described man as being born free but everywhere in chains. But this is not true: everywhere we are born in chains. We begin our lives attached to our mothers – we are far from free. Even the cutting of the umbilical cord is not a moment of freedom; if, as infants, we were left alone and set free, we would die. We are born into family, neighbourhood and nation. These chains – our cultures and traditions – far from choking us, give us the wherewithal to be free.

We need this security, this order, this love, this learning. Home. The child needs to be chained to the values and meaning they are born into in order to be, and feel, liberated. Any curriculum that is imposed on a child should constitute the very constraints the child needs in order to flourish. It should not be personalised to serve the needs of every child. This approach fails because it rejects the importance of the communal experience. Athena has a more important purpose: to introduce the child into our cultural conversations and ways of being. Boundless emotions can enslave us just as much as reason overreaching itself. By recognising the chains that bind us, we can work out which ones hold us up and which ones hold us back.

In *De Magistro* (On the Teacher), St Augustine asked: 'who is so foolishly curious as to send his son to school to learn what the teacher thinks?' It is in the growing freedom from the teacher's thoughts that pupils come to realise their own tastes, develop their own thoughts and make their own judgements. There are no criteria because this is an adventure onto a new plain. A rational liberty through thought, and an aesthetic one through taste and discrimination, is developed via the thoughtful constraints of good curriculum design.

Intellectual life divorced from emotional and physical life is a recipe for dissatisfaction. We need oneness, not the mind divorced from the body. To be truly free we have to accept our natural selves. We are not above these things. Wisdom comes from accepting our conflicted nature. Human reasoning is not a cool, contemplative act; it is rooted in our subjective selves. In order to help make us free, with all our worldly limitations taken for granted, the curriculum must cover all areas – those that confound and confuse as well as those that explain and satisfy. Meaning can be found within the contradictions and different ways of seeing the world that a good curriculum can uncover.

To make more of ourselves and each other, we must have access to the best science and the best art. What human being deserves the worst we have to offer? But what is the best? This can only be answered in the subjective realm, for it is the judgement of humankind that establishes what the best might be at any one time. Therefore, we do not teach the best that has been thought and said; rather, we teach pupils how to make up their own minds, in an informed way, in order to make an educated judgement about what the best might be. The teacher's job is to suggest what is the best, to enlighten, to explore beauty and truth, and to show that while it is sometimes difficult to fathom what the best is, and what it is not, it is necessary to be an informed participant in the conversation.

Chapter 13

To the Things Themselves!

> There is a tendency to seek an objective account of everything before admitting its reality. But often what appears to a more subjective point of view cannot be accounted for in this way ... So either the objective conception of the world is incomplete, or the subjective involves illusions that should be rejected.
>
> Thomas Nagel, Subjective and Objective (1979)

When we are asked to study the best that has been thought and said, we have to assume that we can't objectively know what the best is. We can only know things through our own way of knowing them. Yet some things are clearly better than others. Beethoven's masterful Ninth Symphony *is* better than the tune I made up in the shower earlier, then promptly (and wisely) forgot. My whistled effort might have been the ultimate saviour of humankind, but I doubt it. And if it was, it's now lost to us all. Oh woe!

Our children's first efforts at art might be more at home adorning the family's fridge than hanging next to the Rembrandts and Kahlos in our nation's favourite art galleries. That a child might one day become a celebrated (or neglected) artist is not the point; the work itself has its own qualities. As a parent, we might feel that our child's painting has more importance and meaning to us than the efforts of Matisse, but we wouldn't – unless we are completely lost to the world of sanity – expect that our child's first effort at painting would feature as part of a national curriculum. Instead, we hope that our children are exposed to 'better' art, or even the 'best' art. This judgement *is* necessarily subjective.

Our subjective view of the world is essentially our understanding of it. The curriculum is a collection of things brought together and studied subjectively. The viewpoint of the teacher, the thing being studied and the perspective of the pupils all conspire to make meaning. When a teacher tries to teach something, it is not a magical transference of the same knowing; rather, what is being taught is encountered by the child consciously. What they are conscious of – and how they view it – matters.

Our understanding of consciousness is not merely about being conscious; we are mainly conscious of some 'thing'. We are conscious of the 'things themselves'. The cup of tea in front of me, the view from my window and the words I write on this page are all held within my conscious thought. These words are flowing from my thoughts, but at the same time seem to be surprising me with their expression. 'Ah, so *this* is what I mean …' The cup of tea is in my favourite mug, which is a pleasing colour and is warmly welcome on this very hot day. The view from my window is unexpected as I have recently moved house; it is therefore fascinating because it is not yet familiar. These feelings I have, the way I see things, are articulated by the language I use to categorise and sort these experiences. My attention is being paid to the things within my gaze and the ideas with which I am occupied.

Similarly, a curriculum is a collection of things that we bring to the attention of our children. They then bring their gaze to bear, with varying degrees of attention, on these things. Therefore, the curriculum can be understood in many different ways. The teacher's job is to help their pupils develop a sophisticated palate, a way of knowing the world about them in this moment, as well as the other worlds opening up to them. And we do this by organising our curriculum narratives (our schemas) as complex webs of knowledge organised by values and meaning-making through which we help children to navigate, to experience and to know the world.

Subject teachers introduce different ways of seeing to their pupils. Each discipline has its own perspectives. These domains of knowledge exist in our shared 'lived' worlds; they are culturally mediated and constantly renewed and reforged. Each schema and network of meaning helps the children to appreciate how our ways of seeing, even when we are observing the same things, can be affected by the lenses through which they are viewed. This is where arguments and conflicts may arise, as well as agreements and progress. Recognising that there are different lenses, and appreciating how they each reveal different truths, is the sign of a rich education.

Phenomenology

[Phenomenology means] ... stripping away distractions, habits, clichés of thought, presumptions and received ideas, in order to return our attention to what [Husserl] called the 'things themselves'.

Sarah Bakewell, *At the Existentialist Café: Freedom, Being, and Apricot Cocktails* (2016)

If we strip away all the mechanistic elements of schooling, which are usually couched in utilitarian or utopian terms (target grades, tracking systems, education as a means to social mobility, the job market, etc.), we are left with a focus on the things being studied themselves – the actual content. Imagine that. So much of the machine school approach distracts pupils and teachers from the importance of the stuff being studied. A wise curriculum realises this, which is why we need to refocus our attention on the quality of the content, rather than on the myriad of mechanisms that schools use to measure their way away from deep thought and real learning.

Edmund Husserl (2001 [1900–1901]), one of the most important philosophers on phenomenology, described how life is experienced moment by moment, and that the way we give meaning to our everyday lives is through our encounters with the things of life – phenomena. A curriculum presents children with a wide variety (we hope) of well-chosen phenomena, and although we might wish that they are thought about and remembered by the pupils in the same way that we present them, they are not. How someone understands something is inevitably different from how we might wish it to be understood. For example, you might be nodding along with what I've just written or you might be spluttering objections under your breath.

You might have drifted off entirely, only to be jolted back to consciousness by reading this sentence.

Picasso's *Guernica* could be described scientifically as a collection of materials and pigments, or when experienced through a computer screen as a series of pixels. The painting could be evaluated in a historical context (as a school textbook might want us to understand it) with a few well-chosen remarks about its conception and why it has merit or importance. But an exam board mark scheme might struggle to articulate how a pupil should comprehend the work. Our culture judges *Guernica* to be one of the greatest works of art, but we would find it difficult to impose a unified response because each of us sees it in different ways.

How *Guernica* appears to each of us as an individual is the most important factor for us; however, our viewpoint might be narrow or uninformed – honest but ignorant. For example, our response might derive solely from our ability to discriminate between what we like and what we don't like, and not what is valued and not valued by others. To develop discrimination, we have to respond frankly to our personal responses, but we also need to know how a work is perceived by others, both over time and in the historical context in which it was created.

As the world discloses itself to us, we have to adapt to it, changing ourselves as time goes by. We need to understand that our reactions can be distorted by our ignorance and by the shock of the new. Therefore, we should not be purely reacting to signals from within (to our gut feelings); we should also be acutely sensitive to signals from without. Our social experience of a great painting and all its historical and cultural significance weighs upon us. This is one way in which we may begin to understand it. We receive various viewpoints: how it seems to us, how the teacher describes it, how others have evaluated it, how our peers view it – and all these things can change. In contrast, an input–output model dismisses these elements as inefficient and unnecessary: an explanation is provided, memorised and recalled when needed.

If education is about sagacity, then we want children to be able to approach something new in a way that enables them to access how they feel about it and express their feelings in an articulate manner, as well as appreciating how what they are seeing fits (or doesn't fit) into a wider cultural narrative. We want them to be able to make sense of the world, and themselves within it, as they encounter it. And we want them to understand that something they are not sure about now might be the rock on which they later build a future, so that delaying judgement and having empathy for those with different values and experiences becomes an important part of how they see the world.

Knowledge is infused with our ways of knowing, so the curriculum exists differently in the mind of each and every child. This might have small repercussions for some subjects and be very significant for others. The teacher must understand this unique relationship between child and knowledge because it is central to what takes place in the classroom. We don't just present pupils with information to be learned; we also need to find out how they are viewing this information when they are face to face with the things themselves.

Intentionality

Knowledge is important, obviously. What makes it important is the relationship between the objects, events, thoughts, feelings, moods and ideas being known and the person knowing them. There is no knowledge without the knower. The directedness of the subject knowing (the knower) towards the object being known involves their conscious awareness of the knowledge. The quality of this relationship between mind and world is intentionality or 'aboutness'. Raymond Tallis (2005: 38) writes that 'Intentionality cannot be reduced to causal connectedness of … input–output … it lies at the root of the knowledge relationship and of active inquiry.'

When a parent goes to see a school production in which their child plays the main role, they will watch it in a very different way to the parent whose child was up for the title role but only got a short walk-on/walk-off part. Where internal expectations meet external facts, in this case a school production, there is a fuller story to be told. We become aware of our consciousness when it is directed towards something. The distinction between the inner world and the outer world is made more opaque because both are shared in the mind. Our minds make representations and predictions of the world; without the external world we would be very different animals indeed.

The pure input–output model of education regards the knowledge and the child as somehow separate. The information given is therefore merely 'memorised', rather than representing an interaction between internal (subjective) representation and the external (objective) thing being known. The act of experiencing changes the long-term memory; is not simply a matter of storage because the knowledge and the knower are interdependent. What is known and how it is known: the act of the perceiver in perceiving something comes from their own perspective and experience.

The meanings that we draw about the world are deeply and differently felt. That we are directed towards the world of things is intrinsic to our nature, and curriculum deliberately brings our attention to the things we might not understand. Our curiosity is informed by what we attend to and how we attend to it. If we look at a painting or listen to a piece of music, we are not simply engaged in a reflexive act. We each understand the music differently, we feel it differently, we hear it differently. This reaction is not for all time; as our moods change so can our response. I might be crying one day and laughing the next when I listen to the same piece of music. Or I might have picked this music from my collection for a specific purpose – to lighten my mood or to indulge my melancholia. The music, my mood and my mind are not separate; they are one. The intrinsic and the extrinsic coexist; one does not have dominion over the other.

What we know and how we know it is at once personal as well as culturally mediated by time and place. A school can attend to the overall culture it presents to its pupils, and the quality of its curriculum is an important part of this. What a child attends to alters their mind through the act of attending. Their thoughts, though free, are responding to the environment that we present. Mind = brain + body + environment + community of minds. If we dumb down material to make it accessible, we dumb down the mind attending to it. Where we control the environment we have a responsibility to enrich the minds within it.

Like consciousness and free will, the notion of intentionality is controversial. Some scientists deny that these notions are real, and yet we feel that we come across the reality of them in our everyday lives. According to Franz Brentano's (1973 [1874]) thesis, intentionality is the mark of the mental. For Heidegger, it is 'care' and is shaped by our mood. Intentionality can be thought of as adverbial: I am desiring, loving, hating or believing something, towards which my attention is directed. The fact that when I listen to a piece of music, hear a favourite poem or catch a piece of news or gossip I understand it and perhaps judge it differently to the person next to me is a central aspect of the human experience. The chances are that the next time I hear the melody or the poem I might understand it differently too. After the death of a loved one that poem may take on a different hue. After I fall in love that song means more to me. After I become a parent that piece of news or gossip affects me more profoundly.

Intentionality is not just about how the individual relates to the world. Its intrinsic relevance for the curriculum stems from it being how we collectively view the world. One thing that differentiates us from other animals and from machines is our ability to agree on values, beliefs and modes of meaning, whether these are objects, facts, words or other cultural ways of navigating and changing the world. Alongside our individual intentionality, we have a collective intentionality through which we share an 'aboutness'. This bringing together of individual and collective intentionality is central to the role of the curriculum.

Our consciousness is involved in the world, not independent of it. This means that our personal perspectives are a critical element of our acting-in-the-world. How do we design a curriculum that takes all this into account? Clearly, we can't ignore the viewpoints that children bring with them into the classroom. Some educators argue for a completely personalised experience, yet this fails to make allowance for all that we have in common. The shared space where our different perspectives entwine is an important part of the educative experience. In fact, it is our various ways of seeing that make it imperative that we commune together in classrooms, for this is where we learn the art of conversation and where we share our differing perspectives and experiences.

It is through a communal classroom approach that we recognise our shared humanity and negotiate meaning by learning about the same things at the same time. Inherent in this are the experiences we bring to the classroom, as well as the gradual process of becoming more sophisticated in our ways of reasoning and making judgements, to see if we might agree about the-things-themselves, or at least accommodate a range of different views about them. These multiple viewpoints enable us to pursue wisdom, which has a quality of place and time (the zeitgeist) as well as a personal quality, as it assists us in our continual reorientation to the world and helps us to get closer to an understanding of truth and beauty.

Lebenswelt

Husserl (1970 [1936]) coined the word *Lebenswelt* which translates as 'life-world'. This is the everyday world we are conscious of and make sense of – it is how the world presents itself to us. It coexists in our understanding about what we experience and, crucially, it is a shared space. The world appears to us via networks of meaning. My cup of tea, the clothes I put on, the bus I catch, the bread I buy – these things shape my concept of the world around me. My first- and second-person experience of the world is how I know it. It is the domain in which my knowledge resides.

We form our own truths based on the experience our life-world offers us. It is through our interactions with this life-world that we understand our lives. In this way we come to know each other and ourselves. It is also how we decide on possible changes to make in the world to exercise our control over it to the best of our ability and to create better understandings. Our making and interpreting of knowledge comes to us via this route. Our knowing is not value-free or neutral from the time in which we live. Although much of what we experience is seemingly unconscious, a good amount of it is conscious: it certainly features in my consciousness when my tea is too cold, the button on my trousers falls off, my bus is late or my favourite loaf has sold out.

The rituals and routines, the hidden and explicit curricula of a school, are our attempts – conscious and unconscious – to shape our shared space. This is the life-world of the school through which we make sense of it, of each other, of the knowledge we are learning and of the structures through which we perceive our lives. The 'way we do things around here' leads to cultural fluency: I can exist in this space; it is coherent and known to me. Yet this can also lead to problems when the intrinsic knowledge we hold about how life is becomes so fixed that we can't see how anything beyond it, or different to it, can be right.

Being-in-the-World

Heidegger's *Dasein* (being-in-the-world) is about how we understand ourselves in the world as it is disclosed to us. If we were born into no-world, where we had no-thing and met no-one, what would we be like? These types of thought experiments lead us to the conclusion that we are made biologically, socially and culturally. We do not exist as conscious beings apart from the world; we are not cut off from it; we have no consciousness beyond it. The world is very much part of our consciousness. The world we see is part of what and who we are. What we strive to understand is ourselves in the world. It is through the curriculum that we help children to accomplish this. We are not merely teaching pupils knowledge; we are teaching pupils to be-in-the-world by bringing them into step with the cultural complexities of our time, which, by definition, are established by the traditions they are born into and their engagement with the world as they venture into the future.

We come from no-thing only to return to no-thing. In the meantime, we are flung into the world, not sure that we wholly belong, surrounded by mystery as to the why and knowing that we are resoundingly mortal. Our brief existence makes our being very much part of time. We are temporal creatures, so we understand our world in a temporal way. Whether this is the entire truth of the physical universe does not overly concern us; it is the truth for us.

The fact of our being-in-the-world as honoured guests makes us somewhat angst ridden: we long for belonging. We search for a sense of home and get inklings of what home means to us. We attribute being-here – belonging-to-somewhere – as a glimpse of truth, wholeness, beauty, wisdom, knowing, understanding. How the world makes itself known, and how we come to know the world, is through the subjective perspectives that we bring to it, both through our immediate environment (*Umwelt*) and through a community of others (*Mitwelt*).

This community is known to us through the values, rituals and traditions in which we become involved. Far from being oppressive – as some who call for a more child-centred approach may suggest – the Athena approach to curriculum is about creating a culture of care by structuring ways of being and ways of meaning during a pupil's time at school. This care supports children through a careful exposition of what we are, what we might be, how we live and how we might live.

Our being-in-the-school – a place into which we are flung as much as into life, family, community and groups – makes itself known to us as being-in-this-class-in-this-subject-learning-these-things. It is the very things we learn in the context in which we learn them that helps to give shape and understanding to our lives. Learning is situated in the institution, with the people and in the time in which we study, and, importantly, in the qualities inherent in what we study. The curriculum brings richness to our world. It helps us to explore strange new landscapes and make changes to what we find. It supports us in feeling content with whomever we might meet on the way, and it stirs us into action when we feel the itch for change.

If we are to be wiser about the world, ourselves and each other, about our immediate and wider communities and the community of minds, and if we are to contribute positively, then we need an extensive, qualitative vocabulary and an acceptance that some things are better than others. Without a sense of what is good, what is beautiful and what is wise, we will never aspire to these things in our lives. By finding the better things in our lives, we hope that this will help us know how to live better, both individually and with each other. Although knowledge can also reveal to us that this is not necessarily true.

Knowledge

Knowledge requires not just the brain, or the body, or the engaged body, but an enworlded self.

Raymond Tallis, *The Knowing Animal: A Philosophical Enquiry Into Knowledge and Truth* (2005)

Knowledge is not a neutral set of facts from 'out there' which a teacher tries to transfer into a child's brain. The child is already of the world, as are the teacher and the things being learned. Some things are known and some are vague, so the curriculum can be about clarification – a spiral by which we return to the question, 'How might we see, how might we be?' This pursuit of knowing involves us in finding out information about the world and about ourselves, and, being the creatures who make sense of it all, we clarify the relationship between this new knowing and how we already know the world. We make new webs of connections.

In the shared world, this novel knowledge sometimes results in new understandings about the ways of the world, and sometimes it merely reinforces previously held beliefs. New knowledge that contradicts our previously held beliefs is extremely unlikely to alter how we view the world. Sometimes, this unfortunate trait can mean that we seek out knowledge which reaffirms our beliefs and bolsters our arguments against new knowledge that challenges our viewpoints. David Robson highlights these problems in *The Intelligence Trap* (2019: 263), in which he suggests that 'complex problems … require a wiser way of reasoning, one that recognises our current limitations, tolerates ambiguity and uncertainty, balances multiple perspectives, and bridges diverse areas of expertise'. He calls for 'evidence-based wisdom' which, in school, can arise from a 'complex and challenging curric-ulum' (ibid.: 211).

New knowledge changes the long-term memory. It also changes the world around us: the culture of social media, newspapers and TV, and, accord-ingly, the conversations we have with one another. Memory, which can be highly unreliable, is reinforced and remade by the world in which we find ourselves. And these changes take place in minds that already have ideas of their own (they are not neutral), as well as experiences of the world which support or question that knowledge. This is wisdom: it is the coming together of experience (being-in-the-world), knowledge (finding-out-about-the-world) and judgement (thinking-about-and-action-within-the-world). Our temporality and presence means that we can't sit outside of time and place and see the world as if anew.

Our memory is not a separate, sealed storage unit; it is porous and mallea-ble. In her book *The Memory Illusion*, Julia Shaw (2016: 64) writes: 'while it seems … appealing that every time we recall a memory, we consolidate it and form a stronger and more accurate memory, this is far from the truth. Instead, every time a memory is recalled it is effectively retrieved, exam-ined, and then recreated from scratch to be stored again.' This means that memory is open not just to misremembering but also to manipulation. We can also experience shifts in how we remember things due to changes in the world around us. Treasured memories can become embarrassments or, more helpfully, reforged or forgotten. Our very existence-in-the-world means that we are involved in sense-making because we are part of it. The Athena curriculum helps us to navigate how we might be-in-the-world.

Epoché

According to Sarah Bakewell (2016: 43), 'phenomenology has the capac-ity to neutralise all the "isms" around it, from scientism to religious fundamentalism to Marxism to fascism. All are to be set aside in the *epoché* … This gives phenomenology a surprisingly revolutionary edge.' The goal of setting aside all aspects of the machine approach to education is achievable. Dataism, scientism, targeting, you name it – bracket it out. We can close the door, literally, on those extraneous elements that get in the way of learning. The focus in the classroom should be on the content and the subject matter of what is being taught, which means:

- No target grades.

- No teaching to the test.

- No constant reference to exam criteria.

- No excessive teaching of how to write a GCSE 9-point answer from the age of 11.

- No PEE (point, evidence, explanation) paragraphs.

- No 'easy' or 'accessible' texts or texts chosen for the, often mistaken, instant appeal they might have in engaging pupils.

- No utopian or utilitarian social engineering where the aim is to reduce freedom of thought in order to pursue a narrow agenda.

- No spoon feeding.

- No data tracking in which the child's work is treated as a number which becomes a 'fact' that is 'accurately' measuring their progress.

- No progress as a linear narrative.

- No flight paths.

- No learning journeys.

All these fads should be shut out, with the classroom door acting as the symbolic threshold where the curriculum and human conversation take precedence over everything else. This is a potentially radical act in the current milieu.

In his *Meditations*, Marcus Aurelius wrote: 'The things you think about determine the quality of your mind.' Do we really want a school system in which target setting and pupil tracking distract teachers and pupils from what they are meant to be studying? By focusing on grades over and above learning, many teacher–pupil conversations readily avoid talking about the things themselves. Consequently, the quality of the minds in these schools suffer. When there is an overemphasis on marking criteria, especially when it replaces the thing being learned, the teacher and pupil can spend many a fruitless hour trying to decipher what the criteria might mean or whether the pupil is achieving a target guessed at by the teacher.

Let us imagine three possible conversations:

Scenario 1:

Teacher: You have fallen behind on your target grade. You should be getting a B but in your last essay you got a D. This isn't good enough.

Pupil: I know, sir, I'm sorry. I had a lot of work to do in other subjects and I wasn't able to put the time into the essay I should have.

Teacher: OK. Next time, come to me if you need an extension.

Scenario 2:

Teacher: You have fallen behind on your target grade. You should be getting a B but in your last essay you got a D. This isn't good enough.

Pupil: I know, sir, I'm sorry. What should I have done to make my grade higher?

Teacher: Let's look at the mark scheme. You should have ensured that, for what I estimate a B might be ... Ummm, that you should have expressed 'ideas coherently and with development', whereas you presented 'ideas with some clear topics and organisation'. If you really want to assure a B grade, and maybe aim higher, you might want to 'express ideas with sophistication and sustained development'.

Pupil: Can you give me examples, sir?

Teacher: Er … yes. Well, while you have been clear, you haven't been coherent … Is that clear?

Pupil: Er … I think it's clear, sir, but I'm not sure if it's coherent.

Teacher: Let's settle this by looking up 'coherent' and 'clear' in the *Oxford English Dictionary* … Right, coherent means logical and consistent, is that clear? It's often useful to look at the synonyms – logical, reasoned, rational, cogent, clear … Ah yes, so … anyway, is that clear?

Pupil: I'm not sure, sir.

Teacher: Right, well, let's look up 'clear'. Well, this is clear: . 'Easy to perceive, understand or interpret,' whereas to ensure higher grades you need to be logical and consistent.

Pupil: What are the synonyms for clear, sir?

Teacher: Ah, they are understandable, comprehensible, clearly expressed, logical, lucid, clear-cut, coherent … Right, OK, is that clear? Look, forget this, for the highest achievement you need to express ideas with sophistication and sustained development …

Pupil: What do you mean by sophistication, sir?

Teacher: Dictionary corner … here we go: it means you are 'aware of and able to interpret complex issues'.

Pupil: Should I do that clearly or coherently, sir?

Scenario 3:

Teacher: OK, it seems that you do not quite understand something about the texts we are studying, let me explain it to you …

(Later)

Pupil: Thank you, miss. Sir keeps going on about targets and mark schemes – it confuses the hell out of me. What I like about you is that you address the things themselves. I know what I could write now. [Turns to leave, looks back ...] By the way, what do you think of ... (etc.)

If we look at the intention in each scenario, all three have the same end in mind, which is that the pupil improves, but only one, the third, is clear in this intention. Scenario 1 avoids all discussion of the topic (and in this fictional case the pupil was lying). In Scenario 2, there is no coherent discussion about the topic being learned. Scenario 3 disregards all other concerns and addresses the topic itself.

It is only when the pupil knows what they are talking about that they can hope to decipher what the exam board is asking for. If the pupil knows their stuff and they know how to write an essay properly (which should have been taught throughout their schooling), it should be relatively easy to cope with an exam question – certainly without having to endlessly unpick exam criteria.

In short: bracket out the bullshit.

Chapter 14

The Phenomenological Curriculum

Life is tragic simply because the earth turns and the sun inexorably rises and sets, and one day, for each of us, the sun will go down for the last, last time. Perhaps the whole root of our trouble, the human trouble, is that we will sacrifice all the beauty of our lives, will imprison ourselves in totems, taboos, crosses, blood sacrifices, steeples, mosques, races, armies, flags, nations, in order to deny the fact of death, the only fact we have. It seems to me that one ought to rejoice in the fact of death – ought to decide, indeed, to earn one's death by confronting with passion the conundrum of life. One is responsible for life: It is the small beacon in that terrifying darkness from which we come and to which we shall return.

James Baldwin, *The Fire Next Time* (1963)

The pupil is not merely a lonely individual with a hard skull that needs to be penetrated with a stack of difficult knowledge. Rather, they exist within a network of knowledge that includes their physical body, their idea of themselves, their classmates, their teacher, their culture and the things being studied. All of this adds up to a personal sense of the world and their place within it.

When we are in the classroom we are with others. Having been thrown into this space with a bunch of strangers, how we react to and understand things will be shaped by our sense of self, our companions and the things we encounter. We are not neutral. We are in this world. This sense of being in the life-world is the most important aspect of our schooldays. We are sense-making beings making sense of the world as it is and as it might be.

Those who are with us become part of who we are through a complex web of interactions in the classroom.

We cross boundaries. We interact with where we are, who we are with, what we are studying, how we are studying it and what we are using to study it. In our encounters, we come to realise that mind, body, environment, objects, tools and culture are all intertwined. If we lived in a different world or time or place, our minds would be different. We would be different. To echo Walt Whitman once again, we contain and are part of multitudes.

If we divest ourselves of the idea of the mind as a machine, the brain as a computer made of meat and the act of education as input–output, and instead recognise the subjectivity of each and every one of us, then the relationships between the participants matters. These relationships are teacher–pupil, pupil–pupil and things-being-studied–those-studying-and-teaching-them. We learn in a community of minds.

Fundamental changes take place through these interactions with knowledge and our fellow human beings. Our ideas about wisdom, beauty, rightness, wrongness, love, hatred, foolishness, ugliness – humanity in all its grandeur and all its flaws – are challenged in communion with others. Our preconceptions are modified – some are reinforced and others are undermined – and this brings into focus the fragility of knowing right from wrong. Our need for meaning, by which we anchor our lives, can be upset by the very process of education that gives us meaning and truth. By challenging our thinking, education often alienates the very people it needs to ingratiate – its pupils. How can we come to feel at home in a strange land? We need to connect and be connected.

The mind is not the brain. The mind is most meaningful to us in that it is where we find ourselves. But, of course, without the brain we wouldn't be able to experience the mind. The mind represents an interaction across boundaries. As the philosopher of cognitive science Andy Clark puts it, our higher cognitive self, which operates at a level necessary for the pursuit of wisdom, including reasoning and abstract thinking – the 'classical model', if you will – 'arises at the *productive collision points* of multiple factors and forces – some bodily, some neural, some technological, and some social and cultural'. He adds:

As a result, the project of understanding what is distinctive about human thought and reason may depend on a much broader focus than that to which cognitive science has become most accustomed: one that includes not just body, brain, and the natural world, but the props and aids (pens, paper, institutions) in which our biological brains learn, mature, and operate. (Clark, 2014: 167)

Our mind is affected by the quality of our materials. It is also affected by the calibre of the discussions we have about those materials: how we engage with them, how we approach them and how we interact with them. We then order our thoughts into some semblance of a product which – shaped by cultural expectations and, in turn, responded to socially within those expectations – can surprise. Our minds aren't independent entities; they are part of a whole organism, living and life-full. But they are even more than this.

Clark concludes that the study of the mind includes bodily, environmental and cultural interplay; for him, the mind crosses these boundaries. If you like, it takes a village to raise a child; therefore, the village has a role in developing the qualitative nature of the child's thinking. Imagine a child brought up in a darkened room, with food and drink shoved in through a hatch and excreta taken away through a hole in the floor. This child would be very different to one who is brought up in a caring and vibrant community. The cultural and social traditions and structures we pass on become part of the child's thinking apparatus. How we encourage them to involve themselves in that process, and respond and/or add to it (which is the essence of an education system), is how we help them to construct how they can be-in-the-world.

Embodied and situated cognition – brain, body, action – makes us who we are. Think of the artist and their sketchbook. Their thinking isn't just in their head; it is in the connections between inanimate and unthinking pencil, sketchbook, arm, vision, feeling, judgement, experience and so on which all collude in the 'extended mind'. This interplay makes and remakes the artist they are being. As Alan Jasanoff (2018), professor of biological engineering, brain and cognitive sciences, nuclear science and engineering at the Massachusetts Institute of Technology, puts it:

> … the brain is interwoven with what goes on in the body and the environment … As we seek to understand human conduct, the mystique prompts us to think first of brain-related causes, and pay less attention to factors outside the head. This leads us to … underemphasise the role of contexts across a range of cultural phenomena.

In schools, we provide the context. Teacher and pupils face each other. The 'I' looks at the 'you' and together we form the 'we'. But at any time we can drop out from the 'we' and say 'not me'. We find our home and our enemies in the same place. Some of us wave placards and some of us spit at them. We are at once belonging and not-belonging, safe and disturbed, peaceful and anxious.

But what is this 'we'? It is where our need for mythos and the poetic comes from; it is what helps us to contend with our lot. We need grand narratives because they tell us who 'we' might (and might not) be, but these narratives can be in conflict and we may find ourselves sympathising with many sides of the arguments at the same time. Coming to terms with our conflicted selves is part of the narrative of the curriculum.

Our minds are what we think about, and this 'aboutness' is an interaction between us and us-in-the-world. Has our mind ever *not* been in this world? We connect with the world, and it is through these connections that we make meaning. To be meaningful (full of meaning), it is imperative that we consider the quality of the content we teach because it can offer a way for a child to be. What we teach becomes part of the mind that is being taught. The mind is not static. Its plasticity and predictions are always attending to and drawing on a vast array of information. Our job as teachers is to ensure that the Athena curriculum connects with these active minds. Only connect!

She would only point out the salvation that was latent in his own soul, and in the soul of every man. Only connect! That was the whole of her sermon. Only connect the prose and the passion, and both will be exalted, and human love will be seen at its height. Live in fragments no longer. Only connect and the beast and the monk, robbed of the isolation that is life to either, will die.

Nor was the message difficult to give. It need not take the form of a good 'talking'. By quiet indications the bridge would be built and span their lives with beauty. (Forster, 1910)

Cultural Mobility

[It is] not that they [the books] come alive in him; it is he who lives them.

Walter Benjamin, *Illuminations* (1955)

Curriculum is not injected into a child: it is a peek into the ways a child might live; other modes of being-in-the-world are opened up to them. The ultimate proof of a successful curriculum is for pupils to find themselves able to be at least partially at home in the world. In other words, to understand a number of different environments and/or perspectives. This is cultural mobility – the ability to infer meaning from differing ways of being-in-the-world. Children need to have opportunities to explore a range of art forms, languages, sciences, humanities and so on, and as they traverse they are expanding their minds. As embodied and situated beings-in-the-world, these different cultural environments offer breadth beyond that which a non-educated mind could normally attain. The mind adapts to various ways of seeing the world.

Unlike cultural capital, which sees education as a transactional tool through which we attain 'status', cultural mobility is about how we find various ways to make meaning and reflect on our values and on truth and beauty. Cultural mobility is not about rising up through a hierarchy (like social mobility). Neither is it about perceiving knowledge as a powerful tool for a child to brandish in order to join the bourgeois cultural hegemony. Rather, cultural mobility broadens experience – much like one of the claims that educational sociologist Michael Young (2014: 8) makes for 'powerful knowledge':

> Curriculum (or subject) knowledge is context independent unlike the knowledge based on experience that pupils bring to school … It follows that the task of the teacher… is to enable the pupil to engage with the curriculum and move beyond her/his experience.

I have a great deal of sympathy with Young's concept of powerful knowledge, but there are a couple of areas where we diverge. Firstly, I am concerned by the idea that the curriculum is independent of context because we are contextualised creatures. It is impossible to take away the human perspective entirely – there is no view from nowhere. We can try to be objective, but we cannot be entirely objective because, in understanding and explaining – as well as in posing the question in the first place – we find ourselves responding to our human concerns and contexts.

The second idea I find troublesome is that of a child 'moving beyond' his or her experience. While I understand the sentiment, I worry about denigrating the life experiences of children by valorising the powerful knowledge experiences yet to come. It implies that before a curriculum is experienced, the child is nothing more than a caterpillar (perhaps a hungry one) who needs to become a butterfly in order to move away from its primitive larval existence.

Young's thinking is derived from Durkheim's idea of the sacred and the profane. He is equating knowledge learned at school with the sacred. This knowledge, found in disciplines and subject communities, is taught in schools and is qualitatively different to ordinary everyday knowledge. It enables the child 'to do' and to act on their learning. But why is such a drastic shift required? Why do we need to move beyond? Why not broaden the child's experience of being-in-the-world instead? Much of this felt, ordinary knowledge may be unspoken. It might be difficult to realise its significance but it is still important – and can we really argue that the two 'types of knowledge' do not feed off one another? For example, in the arts, the rupture between ordinary folk knowledge and the powerful knowledge we acquire by moving beyond our personal experience is clearly problematic. Which knowledge is more powerful: B. B. King playing 'Lucille' or a student doing their MA or PhD thesis on the work of B. B. King?

Our daily lives occupy most of our time and thoughts. It is our everydayness – the knowledge of home, of family, of life-as-lived – that provides the security that enables us to contemplate other ways of being-in-the-world. Our knowing doesn't conveniently compartmentalise; it simply adds to and enriches previous knowing or it makes us question it.

Surely, we all have powerful foundations. As such, schools should not be trying to transcend and liberate children from their daily lived experience; rather, we should be imbuing everyday experience with meaning and value. The act of removing human-life-as-experienced from the sphere of knowledge acquisition leads us to downplay the power and necessity of the mythos we are born into, setting it in inferior opposition to more superior knowledge that might make children into 'useful' citizens and culture into a commodity.

For Hannah Arendt, it is the act of a philistine to have 'seized upon them [culture and its objects and artefacts] as a currency by which he bought a higher position in society or acquired a higher degree of self-esteem … In this process, cultural values were treated like … exchange values … They lost the faculty of arresting our attention and moving us' (2006 [1954]: 200–201).

Cultural mobility frees us from the class concerns of social mobility. It is not about assuming a class identity and nor is it hung up on whether we have sold out or no longer belong. Instead of assuming that a person can only have one perspective on the world based on their social standing, cultural mobility accepts that we have more than one way of being-in-the-world. I do not have to reject, or be rejected by, my home, family or culture. Instead, I come to realise that I can be affected by, and adaptable to, different environments and ways of being: in my favourite cafe, at my team's football ground, at work, at play, at home and away. I am different within these environments, but I am not a different person.

As these worlds open up to me, so my mind opens up to them; these worlds disclose themselves to me and I traverse within them, either attuned, or not, to their distinctive qualities. Education should help me to be harmonious with them, and with multiple ways of understanding the world, without inexorably alienating me from my home. Social mobility implies that my origins are a problem, rather than being my anchor and providing my first glimpses of how to be-in-the-world. It attempts to endow me with the cultural capital to put the past behind me. Cultural mobility does not alienate me from my origins.

Knowledge is not power, and nor is it powerful. It is not an exchange or a transaction. Rather, it adds to our way of understanding ourselves in the world and beyond and also within our inner worlds. This is the 'mind' – it transcends borders. Likewise, curriculum is not a list of things to be learned; it is part of our very being. Curriculum helps us to be at home wherever we lay our hat. Curriculum is not about social mobility; curriculum *is* cultural mobility. It opens up a wide variety of perspectives to one and all, building bridges that span lives with goodness, beauty and wisdom, wherever it might be found.

Meaning and Values

At a very young age our children are being encouraged to talk about their individual identities, even before they have them. By the time they reach college many assume that diversity discourse exhausts political discourse, and have shockingly little to say about such perennial questions as class, war, the economy and the common good.

Mark Lilla, The End of Identity Liberalism (2016)

We are born into a culture which already has its ideas on 'the way things are done around here'. Education is one of the ways in which we are socialised in order to participate in the human world. We don't intend to brainwash or oppress children; we want to help them to become themselves in the context of the time and place into which they are born. This is a complex process because in all times and places there are conflicting values, identities and ways of being-in-the-world. We must teach children these different ways of being so they have a chance to choose the grooves in which their lives might attain authentic meaning, and they can thereby make authentic contributions.

This is what an Athena curriculum aims to deliver: it is an insight into what it is to be human, to be 'I' and to be 'we'. The quality of curriculum content matters because it exposes pupils to the knowledge, narratives, values and perspectives that enable them to make meaning in their lives. Instead of identity navel gazing, we are reaching out into the world of possibilities, which are in turn shaped by values.

Teaching knowledge as mere content is not enough: the values and stories that give meaning to knowledge matter too. Schools structure their curriculum narrative through a set of values, both consciously and unconsciously. Some values are inevitably in conflict with others, and therefore represent different ways of knowing the world. To teach through the prism of one set of values does not give children the cultural mobility needed to traverse fruitfully through the world, so a number of ways of seeing and being must be presented and explored.

Subject Disciplines

Schools should be teaching children to confront the conundrums of life-as-it-is-lived. We are not flung into the world as disinterested observers. Curriculum extends our being-in-the-world by presenting cognitive webs in which knowledge, sources, people and ideas come together as systems of understanding. It provides perspectives on ourselves-in-the-world and how we might live within it. Subject knowledge is linked together in a variety of different networks according to certain standpoints. These subject-based perspectives are tied in with values and narratives of thought, which means that teachers situate knowledge within networks of meaning that have been established over time. This is an important feature of formal education. It can never be replaced by Google.

These qualitative ways of understanding are shaped by the values of our culture. Schools should be informing children about different value systems within subjects and also about the great academic clashes over time – showing how they agree, disagree and contradict one another, The children should then be free to find their own values through which to interpret the world.

Curriculum is a dialectical pursuit framed around great narratives. First and greatest among these stories are our subjects – the ways in which we have ordered the academic world for a very long time. These subjects are our great muses. We must not succumb to the doctrine of child-centred learning or a project-based miasma through which children are conned into thinking that they are central to the culture in which they find themselves. Knowledge is not a pick 'n' mix smorgasbord of consumerist passions. Knowledge is understandable only within contexts – for example, words are most useful in sentences, paragraphs, stories and books.

By showing the academic environment as one of excitement – a place where ideas clash and collide – we show that education goes far beyond the exam and into a place where thought enriches the mind.

Colonialism, Content and Culture

Curriculum is anathema to those who believe that our grand narratives have collapsed. Curriculum is all about grand narratives. Curriculum is the poetic making of meaning. It is where the extended chronicles of culture(s) and society(/ies) meet with the local and the individual; the particular with the universal. Without the great narratives, education would be a disjointed set of facts, objects, activities and ideas. That this has been a feature of how some schools have approached curriculum design is understandable. According to Yuval Noah Harari (2018: 261), it is driven by a 'fear of authoritarianism' which has caused teachers to:

... focus on shoving data while encouraging pupils 'to think for themselves' [while having] a particular horror of grand narratives. They assumed that as long as we give students lots of data and a modicum of freedom, the students will create their own picture of the world, and even if this generation fails to synthesise all the data into a coherent and meaningful story of the world, there will be plenty of time to construct a good synthesis in the future ... If this generation lacks a comprehensive view of the cosmos, the future of life will be decided at random.

It is not enough to teach knowledge. Knowledge needs to be framed by meaning, values and argument. We should be engaging pupils in the big ways of seeing the world, not as whole answers (unless these are known) but as perspectives which might just lead us to find glimpses of truth.

Curriculum is about bringing children into contact with some of the grandest narratives of all time: the arts, sciences, humanities, the physical and the metaphysical – the languages through which we make sense of our world. Each subject perspective contributes its own narrative, and together they present the grand narrative which is taught at the altar of Athena: a belief in beauty, truth, care for others and the self, and an absolute focus on the pursuit of wisdom.

For relativists, the pursuit of wisdom is no easy matter. One of their most cogent critiques of curriculum is encapsulated in the question: 'Whose knowledge?' or 'Why is my curriculum male, pale and stale?' Answers to this question can be fraught, and so they should be. This is one of the most challenging and important areas of curriculum design because it immerses us in the conflict between the tradition (the best that has been thought and said) and critical thinking (whose truth?).

Rather than offering us a pat solution, Athena encourages us to bring children into the heart of the conversation. If we take away culture, starve the mind of community and accumulated knowledge, and leave the child with nothing but their own whims, then we reduce their possibilities of being engaged with the world. They have to feel at home in continuity and tradition in order to accept or reject it. Take language: if we fail to introduce children to the linguistic traditions of their culture, their thoughts will be forever diminished as they search desperately not just for a way to communicate but also for a way to think and argue.

Culture is the edifice of our thinking. Our thoughts reach out into the world by means of the world reaching into us through conversation, art, myth, story and science. Our thinking stretches from far beyond us, but so does our discomfort and feelings of not belonging.

What is the point of culture? Culture functions ultimately to ensure the preservation and continuity of a people. In my family, I am the child who is most interested in the story of who we are, in ancestral lands, in our tradition ... But I cannot participate, because Igbo culture privileges men ... If it is true that the full humanity of women is not our culture, then we can and must make it our culture. (Adichie, 2014: 45–46)

Because culture reflects the workings of humankind, wherever we look into culture we will find dispute. The conservative need for home and hearth comes into conflict with those who seek adventure and find home and hearth stifling or discover that it excludes them. The radical and the voice of the 'outsider' are as much a part of our tradition as the staunch defender of the parochial and the status quo.

The tension between the need for home and the desire to break out is central to the idea of culture, family and school. We reject the home provided for us in order to create our own. This can be done with violence or with love, or even a confused mix of the two. As Adichie puts it, how can we both preserve the continuity of a people and also make it 'our' culture if we feel that the past does not support our values and our right to choose how to flourish?

Curriculum, as a series of answers to the questions, 'How do we live?' and 'How should we live?', has to start with the acceptance that we are made by the world as we find it and it finds us. The crucial lesson is that we are shaped both by the natural world and the cultural world. Our freedom comes from our acceptance of being-in-the-world-as-it-is (preservation and continuity) and also from making it our own. We need to make our mark on the world.

Matthew Arnold (2009 [1869]) believed that culture had its origin in the love of perfection, and that it was moved by the force not merely of a passion for pure knowledge but the passion for moral and social good. Terry Eagleton (2014: 130) criticises this view, suggesting that Arnold 'does not seem to recognise that a degree of contention might be involved in the process of making it prevail'. For Roger Scruton (2000: 151), 'only if we teach the young to criticise do we really offer them culture'. By paying homage to great thinkers from the past, our community of minds can appropriate, assimilate, challenge and learn from a variety of perspectives and values.

The study of big themes brings big challenges, but we are the better for it. The great narratives of curriculum are not about dogma; they are about revealing the complexity of human lives in the pursuit of wisdom. Teachers should initiate children into the dialogue so that they too can appreciate the idea of canonical works. The aim is to encourage young people to create works that might, in the future, be deemed to have added to the conversations around what the best might be or continued the discussion about what to include in the canon. Quality, beauty, eloquence, vitality and the sublime can all play their part in the conversation. Children should be able to discuss what pieces of work are 'better' than others and why. They should be able to appreciate arguments for and against a 'great work'. They should be able to add their educated opinion to the ongoing debate.

What matters is that we realise how flexible culture can be and, simultaneously, how important it is to have stability. Culture is given structure by the curriculum so that we can see how tradition changes over time. It is a story with continuity – one that conserves people, language and ideas. In order to challenge it, we must know the value of that which we wish to see destroyed: 'Exactly for the sake of what is new and revolutionary in every child, education must be conservative; it must preserve this newness and introduce it as a new thing into an old world' (Arendt, 1954).

The physical, philosophical and cultural environment into which we are born is within our care. Should we set about annihilating it and ignoring it because we disapprove of it? Should we throw children into the untested, unknown wildness of their own feral imaginations with no structure, no language and no love? Revolution is only possible if we give our children the means to be free of us through a clear understanding of the past and what it represents. If we are forever telling them how they ought to make their world, we fail them. If we refuse to present the world as it is, we fail them. In the spaces between what we say and what we present is where the creative freedom to make their world is to be found.

The Western Education Tradition

I denounce European colonialism … but I respect the learning and profound discoveries of Western civilization.

C. L. R. James, The Making of the Caribbean Peoples (1980 [1966])

We live in one world, and we have to find out what is taking place in the world. And I, a man of the Caribbean, have found that it is in the study of western literature, western philosophy and western history that I have found out the things that I have found out, even about the underdeveloped countries.

C. L. R. James, Discovering Literature in Trinidad (1980 [1969])

To be against 'Western education' is easy. To dismiss a curriculum as white or middle class is easy. But what does this really mean? What do you want to do about it? What does a curriculum look like that is not white or middle class, and – right back atcha – who decides? And once it has been decided, who ensures that it is enacted, and how? The so-called Western education tradition has roots far beyond the geographic West; it involves Muslim scholars and pre-Christian thinkers, and has been continually challenged and added to over the centuries by people who come into the tradition via different ways of engaging with it. It can serve us well because the liberal arts are not set in stone. They are founded on argument and emotion, reason and debate, comparing and contrasting; informing pupils so that they might make up their own minds. The tradition is ever-changing, adaptive and open to absorbing other points of view. However, this does not mean that a curriculum is above criticism. Far from it.

In an Anglo-centric school (in England, for example) the curriculum ought to cover both the British Empire and colonialism. We should not exclude topics on the grounds of ethnic or cultural sensitivity, or else cricket and basketball would not be played in schools because they were invented by dead white men. The theory of evolution, Marxism and post-structuralism would fall by the wayside if we were to focus entirely on the skin colour and genitalia of those who created knowledge in the past. What to bring in and what to remove needs to be thought about in terms of the overall narrative. We must teach about the clash of values and different ways of making meaning because this helps children to comprehend the world. Furthermore, as Alice Walker (2000: 200) puts it, 'healing begins where the wound was made'. If we are even to approach wisdom, we must actively search for different perspectives and understand that each human being has their own unique ways of interrogating the world, which are dependent on their context, their values and their experiences. These perspectives belong in our canon and in our conversations; they help to form our collective intentionality on the world.

When Malala Yousafzai (2013: 136) says, 'Education is neither Eastern nor Western, it is human', we should take note. What we ought not to be doing is universalising the works of white men and ghettoising the works of others. The Western canon includes works picked up and passed on by the Ancient Greeks from places far to the East. It includes all the peoples who have made their home in the West. It includes all the countries the West has come into contact with, through means fair and foul. It includes works from the Mediterranean basin, from Africa and the Middle East. It is a tradition of conquests and winners, opposition and defeat. It ought to include the work of progressives and conservatives, royals and revolutionaries, oppressors and Luddites, individuals and groups, masters and slaves. It is a continuing struggle and discourse, continuing arguments and compromises; it is a continuing dialogue with those who consider themselves to be inheritors of the tradition and those who wish to deny or oppose it, and everyone in-between. The curriculum should not be like the view of history which asserts that it is written by the winners. How we make our curriculum a place where we can all find a home and a meaning for each of us individually, as well as a place in which we can build our community of minds, is something that must be discussed, and decisions made to enable this to happen. Global communication networks mean that opinions can be easily challenged: beliefs can find themselves questioned and people's core values can be dismantled in a single tweet. How do we find comfort when our subjective ways of being-in-the-world become completely relative – no longer about truth and with no overall meaning? Are we all relegated to becoming just another human being passing their time in a meaningless struggle? Relativism is the enemy of meaning; the subjective way of seeing needs direction.

Kwame Anthony Appiah (2018: 207) writes: 'I begrudge nobody the things I love … I can love what is best in anyone's traditions while sharing it gladly with others. Yet if they believe that something in them, some racial essence … connects them with … a geist, that pervades western culture, they understand neither race nor civilisation.' The discussion about what the best might be can cross any cultural barrier that people deem to exist

– quality and meaning is found throughout humanity. It is through culture that we make sense of ourselves and each other, and this is where curricula – and, indeed, civilisations – are made. The conflation of culture and racial or class superiority misrepresents culture; it is there for all.

We also need to avoid placing Western culture on a pedestal whereby it becomes uniquely universalised by virtue of its seeming ability to absorb other cultures. The curriculum which reflected this viewpoint would be merely a collection of disconnected works, rather than a mechanism for providing ways of seeing and being in the world. We need a complex set of connections in order to make the curriculum narrative navigable and to help children make sense of the worlds to which they are being introduced.

To critique any tradition, we need to be able to identify the institutions and thoughts that have contributed to its history, and also to understand that this history is not a seamless narrative of conformity or oppression. All cultures are stories of conflict as well as agreement, both tacit and explicit. Cultures are not homogenous creations. As individuals, we exist within conflicting ways of making sense of the world. We find meaning from socially and economically liberal or conservative viewpoints or any number of different complex webs of thinking, which all need to be addressed and brought into the dialogue. These conflicts occur in everyday culture as lived and also in the more Arnoldian view of canonical 'high culture'. But a great work can create space for us to see beyond the everyday in order to understand the everyday – to understand us in the world.

Some of the greatest works of the canon hold struggle and complexity at their core. In *Culture and the Death of God*, the Marxist cultural critic Terry Eagleton (2014: 55) writes: 'The claim that the literary canon is a bastion of political benightedness … is plainly absurd. The truth is that a good deal of "high" or minority literature is far more politically subversive than most popular culture.' This dabbling in so-called high culture does not mean that schools must become mouthpieces of the Establishment, far from it. Classic works can help to uncover meanings that take our thinking far beyond the everyday and help us to see the world more clearly, more poetically and more thoughtfully. As Italo Calvino (2009: 8) put it: 'A classic is a work which persists as background noise even when a present that is totally incompatible with it holds sway. The fact remains that reading the classics seems to be at odds with our pace of life, which does not tolerate long stretches of time, or the space for humanist otium.'

'Classic books' or 'great books' are, of course, contested terms, but that need not concern us here. I am taking for granted that some books are better than others. I regard great books as great because they enable us to think in new ways, because they open our minds to greater expressions of humanity and our place in the world, and because they undoubtedly belong in the conversation about what the best might be.

If we only fill children's lives with short-lived, populist or accessible works, then they will not be free to understand their world. Contemporary popular culture is readily available, so it need not take up much of our time in school. It has its place, but if we want children to pursue wisdom, then we need to open doors that might otherwise remain closed to them. This means, literally, opening up some great books and other cultural artefacts to reveal canonical knowledge which is difficult but has stood the test of time, in addition to other works which are vying for inclusion in the canon; works which speak to us now in such a way as to connect us to perspectives and meaning in a way that creates pause and reflection, or even a jolt. The safe space of the school is an excellent place for children to explore controversies that will enable them to take part fully in the world. We should ensure that works with which some people might vehemently agree or disagree, like or dislike, are included if their importance warrants it, regardless of personal responses.

Jacques Derrida, the father of deconstruction, said that he only deconstructs texts he loves: 'if deconstruction is only a pretense to ignore ... knowledge of the tradition, it could be a bad thing' (quoted in Olson, 1990: 1). The point is this: we need to love our traditions because they are the space in which we are made. In a piece for *The Guardian*, Priyamvada Gopal (2017) writes:

The British empire ... provides the common ground upon which our histories and identities were forged, whether those be of a white Etonian ... or a queer British Asian female social worker. Between total denial of imperial history and mindless celebration of it comes ... knowledge of what happened. British literature has a great dissident tradition which acknowledges this.

Whether we are a dissident or part of the establishment, we are thrown into space and time – a mutual place which helps to make us who we are. Culture implies rootedness – a growing from the soil that connects blood and land. Fascistic undercurrents have long since put this idea beyond the pale, but the pull of home is and will remain real. People have long been enriched by the cultural activities of diaspora communities, where rootedness is not fixed to the land but plays out through culture as different modes of meaning. There is a deeply felt pull to somewhere, to an idea of home, but it is continually adaptable. It is not dominated by a fixed root but by an organic tradition that adapts to us as we adapt to it.

When we come together as a community of minds we might find harmony, but we might also find argument and disagreement. This can be due to differences in our values and identity as well as, too often, belligerence or prejudice. This is why, as I suggest in *Trivium 21c* (2013), exploring these areas of conflict, contrast and schism is hugely important. Sometimes these juxtapositions can be extreme and dangerous, such as when reactionary forces try to sow discord, but more often than not they enable us to expand our perspectives on the world, to make judgements about various issues in our lives: politically, socially, aesthetically and even seemingly mundane decisions, such as what to have for lunch. How we negotiate, empathise with and argue about values begins in the first community of minds we have access to beyond our immediate family and friends – school. It is school which brings direction to our viewpoints as we are brought face-to-face with the perspectives of others, particularly those who are more wise than we are. Athena becomes our guide.

Dialectic

Roberto Unger said: 'we have to struggle for a different form of education … It should be radically dialectical in its approach; every subject should be taught at least twice from contrasting points of view' (Wood, 2014). The beauty of the trivium model is that it gives space for dialectic: discourse and argument, understanding and empathy. It is the clash of values that matters, rather than simply counting numbers of representatives or groups, so values must be represented in the curriculum narrative. We need to deliberately offer different perspectives in order for pupils to begin to see that some things to be learned about are contested. Seeing different issues from different viewpoints means that children can begin to build on their value systems and see how others build on theirs. Far from sowing discord for the sake of it, these clashes of values can bring agreement as well as respect for differing views – and without falling into the relativist trap in which all viewpoints are perceived as having equal value.

Interestingly, much of the science about how we learn and remember supports this approach. The work of Robert and Elizabeth Bjork, from the UCLA Learning and Forgetting Lab, suggests that some of the best ways of remembering include interleaved practice and inductive learning. For example, the Bjorks propose that interleaving two or more paintings by different painters, and alternating between them, can improve the retention and transferability of knowledge about the artists' style. Subsequently, participants in the Bjorks' research were able to discriminate between artworks they hadn't seen before, correctly identifying which painting had been produced by which painter.[1] These strategies not only impact on curriculum design, but they also emphasise how a dialectical approach to curriculum design can aid learning.

Discerning between one thing and another is essential when it comes to meaning. This is where inductive learning comes into its own. (Inductive learning involves pupils looking for patterns and differences; using inference and drawing on evidence is an essential part of the process.) How do

---

[1] See https://bjorklab.psych.ucla.edu/research/.

we know the animal in front of us is a cat? How do we know it is not a dog? Which is the cat and which is the dog? The Bjorks ask: how do we distinguish a malignant tumour from a benign one or differentiate between a Monet and a Van Gogh painting?

The ability to discriminate naturally leads to arguments – from the aesthetic to the political: which is more intelligent – cat or dog? Who is the best painter – Monet or Van Gogh? Which political party will form the best government? Education that juxtaposes different ways of seeing and knowing helps pupils to begin to understand how they might develop their knowledge, taste and opinions, while at the same time appreciating how others interpret the same things differently. By looking for the best, the worst and the points in-between, and exploring all the contradictions, a fuller education can be had.

A dialectical process is a necessary part of an education in the pursuit of wisdom. We add qualitative ideas to the mix and discuss their distinguishing features. We examine history, philosophy, art and science in this way. The whole curriculum is based on returning to ideas of ever more complexity and building up ways of knowing through and across subjects. By comparing and contrasting work, understanding values-based approaches and recognising how different perspectives can lead us to arrive at different conclusions, teachers and pupils are more able to make qualitative judgements about the work they study as well as the work they produce.

Wisdom

Bringing the human back into the picture means jettisoning the paraphernalia and instrumentalism of the Machine. Knowledge is not a means to an end; it is the thing itself. Knowledge improves us by setting us off on a quest for wisdom. This pursuit can only ever be based on the human being-in-the-world in which the self – along with our beliefs, experiences, values and stories – shapes the mind. This knowledge gives context to the knowing of new things and is brought into play through judgement, taste, discernment and freedom. It is important for children to be, and become, enriched as a result of coming into contact with the great work of great people and the great work of flawed people. It is important for them to encounter the work of artists and writers regardless of their skin colour or gender, but also to realise that there are reasons why the canon includes the works it does and that this is controversial and should continue to be addressed. What is taught in schools is just the beginning of a lifelong conversation. Breadth is important because context enables us to understand more, in the long term, than an in-depth exploration of a few disconnected things.

From Augustine to Arendt to Angelou, there are great 'souls' who should be celebrated because they are part of the great tradition – but a malleable tradition that can be altered by today's teachers for the children of tomorrow. The experiences of pupils are augmented; new webs of knowledge are organised by competing values, narratives and patterns; and meanings in time are offered in such a way as to develop the exercise of free will through the opportunity to make judgements, arguments, comparisons and connections.

Approaches to curriculum design must always have a philosophical underpinning as well as an understanding of how research, institutional pressures, teacher capabilities, pupil and parent expectations, and societal demands and pressures might impact on the pragmatic decisions that have to be made. I hope I have successfully argued that a curriculum that is sensitive to the pursuit of wisdom is a very different beast to one that just serves the Machine. Inevitably, the curriculum in each school will be different (I don't think it's wise to buy an Athena curriculum 'off the peg') because it will be finely tailored to suit the school and its context.

So, how this might be done?

The Athena Approach to Curriculum Design

Context, growth, coherence, dialectics and collaboration all come together in a joined-up vision, where curriculum is the progression model and where pupils' experiences and judgements bring to life the knowledge they are learning. This approach adds to my writings elsewhere on the trivium (Robinson, 2013), which I firmly believe provides a firm base for those who wish to introduce a curriculum that goes beyond delivering graded outcomes.

What follows are a few ideas as to some things schools might be thinking about doing and how they can be included in an overall approach to pursuing wisdom in the curriculum.

Curriculum Coherence

A curriculum should make sense. This might seem an obvious statement – who, after all, would pursue a curriculum that did not make sense. Yet, it is possible to end up with an incoherent curriculum if certain factors are not in place, though this must not ignore its necessary complexity.

Firstly, the curriculum needs to be joined up – like a well-crafted narrative, there needs to be a sense of how it all hangs together. Secondly, every teacher needs to be aware of the narrative – the parts of it they are teaching and how it fits into the overall structure. Thirdly, the pupils need to understand this narrative – they should to be able to detect an underlying logic and engage with its unfolding. Fourthly, assessment should be used to ascertain how well the narrative is being understood and also to help communicate and embed it. The schools inspectorate in England, Ofsted (2018), sum this up as 'intent, implementation and impact'.

The curriculum is not well thought out if teaching is completely autonomous. It is not coherent if there is teaching to the test or if certain parts of the curriculum are given less focus – for example, if Key Stage 3 is little more than a stopgap rather than an essential part of the narrative. The curriculum does not hang together if a child is unable to understand and express, with at least a degree of coherence, how things connect to other things – for example, how new information might fit into an existing schema. Assessment won't work if it is all about progression statements that bear no relationship to what is being studied and when.

To ensure that curriculum coherence is an ongoing task, each subject area needs to have enough freedom to be true to their discipline, but also to be guided by the school's overriding ethos and values. At the school level, curriculum coherence must not suffocate teaching, but instead should allow it to breathe freely by being adaptable enough for each subject area to be taught wisely.

The T-shaped Curriculum

Organisational principles – the grand narratives that hold together the ideas, issues and insights that subjects can offer us – can be structured through a T-shaped curriculum: the horizontal line of the T represents breadth (context) and the vertical line represents depth (specific detail).

In *A Short History of Europe,* Simon Jenkins writes:

I disagree with syllabuses that maintain history is better taught in depth rather than breadth. Depth should follow breadth, for without it history is meaningless. Without awareness of the timeline of human activity, individuals become dissociated figures on a bare stage. Those who cannot speak history to one another have nothing meaningful to say. Context – which means a sense of proportion – is everything. (Jenkins, 2018: 5)

A knowledge-based curriculum could easily become a list of facts, but an Athena curriculum sets knowledge in context. This can be extremely broad – and, yes, it can cross subject boundaries (think of modernism or the Renaissance, for example), it can be concept-oriented and it can be values-driven. Without breadth, depth can be left bereft. The need for meaning drives the pursuit of perspectival seeing. Think how a Marxist or a Libertarian might view a work of art or a moment in history. Now consider how a pupil might cope in an English literature class faced with Mary Shelley's *Frankenstein,* having never explored what a novel is and with no understanding of the Gothic or romanticism and their relationship to the Enlightenment. No wonder they rely on spoon feeding. Meaning needs to be seen in context. Moments in time shape thought, as do the communities of thought in which creators find themselves as they shape their contributions to the conversation(s) that, eventually, find their way into our curricula.

The Spiral Curriculum

In *The Process of Education,* Jerome Bruner (1960: 13) wrote: 'A curriculum as it develops should revisit ... basic ideas repeatedly, building upon them until the student has grasped the full formal apparatus that goes with them.' This idea is central to the spiral curriculum which is focused on meaning, values, perspectives, experience and judgement.

In every subject there are ideas, concepts and foundational knowledge on which the subject studied is built (for example, Empire and colonialism, revolution, drawing, painting, sculpture, the novel, poetry, sauces and gravies, particles, cells, staging, physical and mental well-being). We might argue about some of these ideas, and so we should, but the point is to ascertain what the organising principles around which a subject curriculum might flow are, because these basic ideas recur.

If we think about painting in an art curriculum, we know that it covers a lot of different techniques, tools, pigments, styles, eras, artists and so on. Each time we revisit painting, we learn more about painting as a whole as well as about the particularities of painting being taught at the time. It would be ridiculous to teach painting once and never return to it. By spiralling back later, the learning is reinforced. If we take into account forgetting as a way of forging better learning, it seems sensible to keep returning to and building on what was done before, rather than leaving it so long that it has been completely forgotten or so lost in the mists of time as to be difficult to resurrect. 'We do painting in the autumn term of Year 7' doesn't really cut it.

What are the organising principles, ideas, concepts, precepts and pieces of foundational knowledge in the subject you teach? A knowledge-rich curriculum can be built around these, and, in so doing, it will ensure good retention, good thinking, good joined-up-ness, good progress and a curriculum in which the central narrative(s) and tenets are clear.

Intelligent Interleaving

Interleaving can be utilised as a practice method – for example, in maths, a multiplication problem followed by a division sum, followed by trigonometry and so on – or it can be part of an approach to curriculum design, whereby content is deliberately juxtaposed to improve understanding. This latter form of interleaving can be done thoughtlessly – anything can be interleaved with something completely unconnected. But when two or more elements of curriculum content are deliberately chosen because they juxtapose well, and/or offer interesting viewpoints and perspectives, it helps children to develop and exercise their values, beliefs and arguments. Comparing and contrasting assists understanding. 'Which do you prefer – this taste or this taste? Perhaps you need to appreciate this flavour which seems to have passed you by ...' By addressing the subjective viewpoints that pupils bring into the classroom, we enable them to develop more sophisticated palates. When I teach drama, I interleave Brecht, Stanislavsky and Artaud. We start by discussing how each practitioner has a different view about truth and its representation, and then go on to consider how their ideas compare and contrast theoretically and practically. By studying them alongside each other, the pupils not only get a much richer view of theatre, but they are also clearer in their minds about what each individual practitioner's style is like and why.

As mentioned above, interleaving in art enables pupils to compare and contrast earlier and later works by the same artist or works by different artists in similar or contrasting styles. In literature, poetry can be compared to prose or two poems can be juxtaposed. In politics, Thomas Paine can be read alongside Edmund Burke. The lessons can be spaced apart in chunks of two or three or they can alternate. As the pupils' knowledge becomes more secure they can compare and contrast in the same lesson. Alternatively, lessons can begin inductively – the works are presented alongside each other and the pupils learn to differentiate, looking for commonalities and differences from the off.

Intelligent interleaving allows pupils to develop their abilities to discriminate. In the case of the three theatre practitioners, the pupils developed their ability to decide which style they liked best and why. The qualitative judgements they were beginning to make then enabled them to look at their own work more critically. Interleaving is about juxtaposing material which has significant connections: the material should benefit from being studied in tandem with other pieces precisely because there is a shared commonality which benefits from comparing and contrasting.

Collaboration

One of the best things about being an independent-minded teacher is that you can sit in meetings, smile and nod away at all the latest initiatives, work out how to pay lip-service to them and then go about your merry business in the usual way. The potential for mavericks to do it their way is huge, which is why some more martinet managerial types will use a variety of means to make sure that the awkward squad are brought to heel. Lesson observations, scripted lessons, book checks, planning checks, interviewing pupils – all these measures and more might be used to bring the radical into line.

The awkward teacher, even when told to work chapter by chapter from a textbook, can go off-script as soon as the classroom door closes. They don't do this to be a bad teacher; they do it to be a better one. Perhaps the textbook on its own is not enough or the lesson plans are past their best or were never part of a joined-up sequence. The teacher alone has the key to the kingdom of knowledge for their kids and should have an absolute belief that they can unlock the wonders of wisdom.

The maverick teacher can blossom when it comes to curriculum design because good curriculum design is a collaborative affair. The essential element is how it all connects together. A wise school invests in giving teachers time to work together to create a curriculum in which they all have a say. What knowledge, when, how to teach it, what the children should be producing, how to assess it, how to review it, how to change it and tweak it – all this is part of the continuing, unfinished project of good curriculum design. Utilising the creativity of teaching staff to create a joined-up curriculum ensures that it has buy-in from the teachers, who can then take responsibility for its successes as well as any problems that may occur en route.

Rebellious teachers may still go off-piste, but they will be more aware of how and where they fit into the whole curriculum and how essential it is that they pass the baton on to their colleagues so that others can run with it.

Curriculum design must be sensitive to individuals' perspectives and values, because without this subjective sensibility it can become a cynical and mechanical mode of delivery for off-the-shelf agendas. In each school (or cluster) and in each department, the voices of teachers must ring out loud and clear – their perspectives and beliefs, their text selections, their contexts, the narratives they wish to tell.

The teacher's primary job when designing a curriculum is to help their pupils find meaning in the world, to reflect on their values and to find ways of being-in-the-world via an understanding of beauty, the sublime, universal truths and a realisation that they too can become part of the ongoing conversation. Universal truths might be glimpsed in Greek tragedy or in the teachings of Euclid and Archimedes. It might be present in the works of Confucius, the pages of the *Mahabharata*, the stories of the *Arabian Nights*, the works of Shakespeare and Dante, the paintings of da Vinci and Picasso, Van Gogh and Hockney. It might also be present in the words and deeds of Sappho, Greer, Behn, Hepworth, Austen, Brontë, Shelley, Wollstonecraft, Boudicca, Dickinson, Curie, Luxemburg, de Beauvoir, Stein, Friedan and Paglia. Whichever rich sources teachers choose, as long as these choices are made with a rich narrative in mind, rather than a cynical 'This will be sufficient to enable our kids to do OK in the test,' then all will be well.

The guiding light should be Athena: what is the wisest thing to teach? What is the wisest way to teach it? What will most likely open up wisdom for the child and the adult yet to be? No other considerations need be entertained.

A good curriculum is a place for the richness and diversity from thousands of years of tradition and conflict to sing. A place for sceptical voices and for those who say 'no!' A place for dialectical difficulties, for weighing up values, for discernment about beauty, for pursuing truth and for new meanings to emerge in the minds of pupils inspired by the stories that continue to either cement or critique the tradition, re-evaluate it or look to alternative traditions – or, indeed a mix of all these possibilities. Some of these issues might be more acute in the humanities and the arts than in maths and the sciences, but there are arguments and perspectives throughout all areas of curriculum design. Pupils need to gain experience and knowledge and begin to exercise their freedom of judgement, but we must be careful that freedom does not collapse all narratives into meaningless chaos. Meaning is key.

Chapter 15

Making Meaning

A striking conclusion that we have drawn from the findings is that, despite the fact that the curriculum is what is taught, there is little debate or reflection about it ... there is a lack of clarity around the language of the curriculum.

It is certainly possible that this ambiguity and lack of shared understanding expose competing notions of what curriculum means across the sector. However, the most likely explanation is that this arises from a weak theoretical understanding of curriculum ... Over time, this competence across the sector [has] ebbed away.

Amanda Spielman, HMCI's Commentary: Recent Primary and Secondary Curriculum Research (2017)

In Part I of this book, I introduced the office school – a place where a form of machine thinking has taken over from the desire to educate. The system accrues data which charts pupil progress. Everything is chained to this progress. There is less desire to get down and dirty with narratives of knowledge than there is to offer shiny slogans of mediocre mindset accomplishments to motivate children to become socially mobile. Education is about grades, and grades are capital that young people can exchange for more courses and/or jobs. At the same time, they are faced with a future that well-meaning people with limited minds have mapped out for them.

Utility and utopia are the basis for this type of education. Tied into corporate interests and a quasi-liberal dream factory, it is no surprise that global businesses tap into this vision. They too offer utopia, although this utopia is destined for your classroom. The branding and slogans are part of the 'one vision' approach to schooling. Do one thing well – but make sure it is measurable and can adorn a letterhead. In order to keep everyone in check, a strong hierarchical structure (reliant on measuring what can be measured) endeavours to preserve some semblance of progress and intervention. Whether the measurements are valid matters less than the fact that the data is collected. At the same time, technology is embraced as a good in itself. Mechanical metaphors abound: the teacher as robot and the mind as a machine made of meat. All schools have to do is become efficient at transferring knowledge so that higher grades ensue and, hey presto, our children become socially mobile adults who make for a better, fairer world.

But as we have seen, schools are large and contain multitudes. The unidirectional approach leads to casualties, of which wisdom is one. Knowledge – when it is merely accumulative and acquired for a single end-point, especially when that end is a percentage – is not about accruing wisdom. Knowing is more important than numbers. Somewhere in-between the transfer of a piece of knowledge and its storage in long-term memory, a person looks on. At the centre of the objective transaction there is an individual with their own slant on the knowledge being taught and retained and how valuable they think it might be. Whether the Machine likes it or not, there are human subjects gazing into the world, conscious of what they see but unconscious of why they are conscious.

It matters how this human subject begins to understand the world. Curriculum represents the purposeful way in which a school interacts with its pupils, and meaning comes through the wisdom of that curriculum. The better the quality of the interaction, the greater the chance that a young person can arrive at meaning which has depth, quality and wisdom.

Central to our concern is not merely knowledge transfer but meaning-making: how a child understands the world and finds their place within it. Meaning is made by each individual in their own personal pursuit, but this pursuit is bound up in the social, environmental and cultural settings in which they find themselves. It is enhanced by interactions with family, friends and institutions, each impacting consciously and unconsciously on the child. This subjective, poetic world is the greatest gift a school can bestow. It is arrived at through conversations between child, teacher and text, and where experience and authority come into dialogue with naivety and possibility. Each offers insights. Truth, beauty, doubt and uncertainty all guide us on our well-worn path.

It is because the world of education is so reliant on different perspectives that the quality of these perspectives is so important. The post-modern enthusiasm for relativism is waking up to a world where fake news and alternative facts are undermining truth and wisdom. Schools are pivotal in providing the foundations for the debate. They are part of the public space where comparisons of quality and truth are glimpsed and then discussed, so that we arrive at a set of values which, in turn, give meaning and structure to our lives.

Maybe it is the image of the Goethe-reading, Wagner-appreciating SS officer that did so much damage to the idea that education in the finer things – Matthew Arnold's pursuit of perfection and 'sweetness and light' – might make someone into a better person. A well-educated individual is not necessarily a better one. Yet, if rather than floundering their way into wrongness, a pupil at least understands that some things are more right, more true and more valuable than others, then at least they will have made their choices based on a set of values rather than on a supra-belief in the ego as the sole arbiter.

An Athena education is resistant to utilitarian, managerial, instrumental, vocational and simplistic utopian arguments about why we educate. Knowledge for its own sake is anti-utility and anti-training. It is against the idea of knowledge as cultural capital or literacy. It resists the ideas of knowledge for social justice or social mobility. This knowledge is not power, and nor is it powerful. Instead, it is human scaled – it modestly helps us to understand who we are, and who we might be, by engaging the subjective ways of being in our shared world.

This impacts on the choices we make for a curriculum in which there is an emphasis on the pursuit of truth. This truth is to be found in great books, authentic experiences and a discursive/dialectical method of teaching. In this way, children learn important knowledge. They have great experiences – cultural, physical and thoughtful. They learn to think about how they interact with what is being gifted to them. They converse, debate, write, make speeches, play sport and make art. They learn other languages for the joy of having their minds expanded by different ways of seeing and interpreting the world. They learn science to explore the wonder of the world. Through the breadth of these academic experiences – or, as Arnold (1964 [1868–1882]: 300) called it, 'the whole circle of knowledge' – children are expected to learn the importance of truth and that there are different ways to find truth; some more objective and logical; some more subjective, spiritual and emotional.

The Athena curriculum has a moral imperative. It is taught through the trivium method: important and beautiful ideas and objects are introduced through teacher-directed talk; then through dialogue, debate and discussion; and then through the pupils creating their own responses to drive the conversation forward. The essay form is central, as are other means of subject-specific communication. The dialectical approach at the heart of the trivium model gives us important insights into how to structure a curriculum – for example, intelligent interleaving, inductive techniques, offering perspectives, weighing up arguments, and examining evidence and subjective viewpoints are all essential.

The sequencing of knowledge is vital. It is all about building up an understanding of how different disciplines work together. Domains are extremely important, so an Athena approach requires the teacher to be an expert in their field. They are the sage on the stage and they stand on the shoulders of giants who, over time, have made each domain what it is today. The question 'What knowledge?' is keenly felt. What knowledge to teach is informed by the traditions, arguments and conversations in each domain. That this might be a result of arbitrary historic practices doesn't really matter. These seemingly arbitrary responses were the result of us connecting us to and thinking about the world: among these responses wisdom is found. What does matter is that an Athena curriculum will recognise the controversies at its heart and seek out the wise. For example, an economics curriculum ought to include both Adam Smith and Karl Marx. If it didn't, it would fail to introduce pupils to one of the great debates in economics, and thus would restrict their ability to take part in well-informed conversations in that domain and thus find a way forward.

It is essential for children to learn how to make meaning in the world. None of our lenses is definitive: there are only incomplete perspectives, each of which has its own theories and value systems. Because we want children to understand these different ways of seeing, we must teach them – in the context of subjects (and sometimes across subjects) – how the great ways of understanding link the arts, technology, history, beliefs and how we live our lives. We teach dialectically to open up a dialogue as to how we have lived and how we might live, and to explore the why – the meanings, values and judgements that help to make us who we are.

Epilogue

[M]achines only have the chips, humans have the heart. So I think we have to change from now on the education system ... If you think like a machine, the problem will come. In the past twenty years we made people like machines. In the next twenty years machines will look like people. So in the future, it's not knowledge-driven, it's wisdom-driven, it's experience-driven.

Jack Ma, Education is the Biggest Challenge (2018)

Even Jack Ma, executive chair of the Alibaba Group, a multinational technology conglomerate, can see that there is a problem with machine thinking. And, of course, those imbued with anti-capitalist revolutionary fervour, such as Paul Mason, share his concerns. Mason (2019: 273) proposes small acts of rebellion to refuse 'machine control', suggesting that this 'micro-scale resistance will lead us towards a society-wide project'.

If you were to visit an Athena school, would it be noticeably different? Well, there would be no crowing about statistics and instead a celebration of things that are known, knowable and even mysterious. There would be great art, drama, music, dance, design, histories, geographies, languages, philosophies, religions, sciences and mathematics. Each department would feel different because each is an upholder of a great tradition, but each would also share in the overall project by offering perspectives in the pursuit of wisdom.

The Athena school is a human space. The job of a school is not to expand the realm of the Machine but to expand the realm of the human. Quality matters – and not just any old knowing will do. If we are to live exuberantly in the technological age that we seem destined to become a part of, then we need to be at our most human.

Lawrence Stenhouse (1975: 82) wrote: 'Education enhances the freedom of man by inducting him into the knowledge of his culture as a thinking system,' and suggested that 'Education as induction into knowledge is successful to the extent that it makes the behavioural outcomes of the students unpredictable.' This is what we need to bear in mind when designing a curriculum. We are not presenting a journey with a destination; we are opening up a number of perspectives and narratives through which a child can make the most of their life. Furthermore, it will help them to raise their own children in a way that values the cultures of the world into which they, too, will be born.

An Athena school is a transcendent space imbued with the stuff of culture. This culture involves us writing ourselves into the mythos because the mythos helps us to engage with the truth.

Athena is the mythos for all wise schools. Athena gives us the why.

When philosophy paints its grey in grey, one form of life has become old, and by means of grey it cannot be rejuvenated, but only known. The owl of Minerva takes its flight only when the shades of night are gathering.

Georg Wilhelm Friedrich Hegel, *Philosophy of Right* (1821)

The shades of night are gathering around the mechanistic approach to schooling. It is now time to let Athena's owl fly.

Bibliography

Adichie, Chimamanda Ngozi (2014) *We Should All Be Feminists*. London: Fourth Estate.

Allen, Rebecca (2018) What If We Cannot Measure Pupil Progress?, *Rebecca Allen* [blog] (28 May). Available at: https://rebeccaallen.co.uk/2018/05/23/what-if-we-cannot-measure-pupil-progress/.

Angelou, Maya (1994) *The Complete Collected Poems of Maya Angelou*. London: Virago.

Appiah, Kwame Anthony (2018) *The Lies That Bind: Rethinking Identity*. London: Profile Books.

Arendt, Hannah (1954) The Crisis in Education. Available at: https://www.digitalcounterrevolution.co.uk/2016/hannah-arendt-the-crisis-in-education-full-text/.

Arendt, Hannah (2006 [1954]) *Between Present and Future*. London: Penguin.

Arendt, Hannah (2006 [1963]) *Eichmann in Jerusalem: A Report on the Banality of Evil*. New York: Penguin.

Arnold, Matthew (1964 [1868–1882]) *Schools and Universities on the Continent*, ed. R. H. Super. Ann Arbor, MI: The University of Michigan Press.

Arnold, Matthew (2009 [1869]) *Culture and Anarchy*. Oxford: Oxford World's Classics.

Augustine, St (389) *De Magistro* (On the Teacher). Available at: http://www.nyu.edu/classes/gmoran/augustine.pdf.

Augustine, St (397–426) *De Doctrina Christiana* (On Christian Doctrine). Available at: http://www.intratext.com/IXT/ENG0137/.

Bakewell, Sarah (2016) *At the Existentialist Café: Freedom, Being, and Apricot Cocktails*. London: Chatto & Windus.

Baldwin, James (1963) *The Fire Next Time*. New York: Dial Press.

Benjamin, Walter (1999 [1955]) *Illuminations*, tr. Harry Zohn. London: Pimlico.

Berlin, Isaiah (1953) *The Hedgehog and the Fox*. London: Weidenfeld & Nicolson.

Berlin, Isaiah (1999) *The Roots of Romanticism: The A. W. Mellon Lectures*. Princeton, NJ: Princeton University Press.

Berlin, Isaiah (2008 [1977]) *Russian Thinkers*. London: Penguin.

Bloom, Adi (2018) Thousands of Teachers Are On Long-Term Stress Leave, New Figures Reveal, *TES* (11 January). Available at: https://www.tes.com/news/thousands-teachers-are-long-term-stress-leave-new-figures-reveal.

Bloom, Allan (1987) *The Closing of the American Mind*. New York: Simon & Schuster.

Brentano, Franz (1973 [1874]) *Psychology from an Empirical Standpoint* (Psychologie vom empirischen Standpunkte), tr. Antos C. Rancurello, D. B. Terrell and Linda L. McAlister. London: Routledge & Kegan Paul.

Bronowski, Jacob (2008 [1951]) *The Common Sense of Science*. London: Faber & Faber.

Bruner, Jerome (1960) *The Process of Education*. Cambridge, MA: Harvard University Press.

Burke, Edmund (1899 [1790]) Reflections on the Revolution in France, in *The Works of the Right Honourable Edmund Burke*, Vol. 3. London: John C. Nimmo.

Calvino, Italo (2009) *Why Read the Classics?* London: Penguin.

Caplan, Bryan (2018) *The Case Against Education: Why the Education System is a Waste of Time and Money*. Princeton, NJ: Princeton University Press.

Cappelli, Peter and Tavis, Anna (2016) The Performance Management Revolution, *Harvard Business Review* (October). Available at: https://hbr.org/2016/10/the-performance-management-revolution.

Cave, Stephen (2016) There's No Such Thing as Free Will, *The Atlantic* (June). Available at: https://www.theatlantic.com/magazine/archive/2016/06/theres-no-such-thing-as-free-will/480750/.

Chambers (1988) *Chambers Dictionary of Etymology*, ed. Robert K. Barnhart. Edinburgh: Chambers.

Chen, Ying and VanderWeele, Tyler J. (2018) Associations of Religious Upbringing with Subsequent Health and Well-Being from Adolescence to Young Adulthood: An Outcome-Wide Analysis, *American Journal of Epidemiology*, 187(11): 2355–2364. Available at: https://academic.oup.com/aje/article/187/11/2355/5094534.

Clark, Andy (2014) *Mindware: An Introduction to the Philosophy of Cognitive Science*, 2nd edn. New York: Oxford University Press.

Clark, Andy (2016) *Surfing Uncertainty: Prediction, Action, and the Embodied Mind*. New York: Oxford University Press.

Collins, Anita (2015) Music Education Key to Raising Literacy and Numeracy Standards, *Sydney Morning Herald* (6 June). Available at: https://www.smh.com.au/education/music-education-key-to-raising-literacy-and-numeracy-standards-20150605-ghhuw9.html.

Congreve, William (1697) *The Mourning Bride*. Available at: http://talebooks.com/ebooks/557.pdf.

Covey, Stephen R. (2004) *The Seven Habits of Highly Effective People: Powerful Lessons in Personal Change*. New York: Free Press.

Cunningham, Lillian (2015a) Accenture CEO Explains Why He's Overhauling Performance Reviews, *Washington Post* (23 July). Available at: https://www.washingtonpost.com/news/on-leadership/wp/2015/07/23/accenture-ceo-explains-the-reasons-why-hes-overhauling-performance-reviews/?utm_term=.a61d001905c0.

Cunningham, Lillian (2015b) Accenture: One of World's Biggest Companies to Scrap Annual Performance Reviews, *The Independent* (28 July). Available at: https://www.independent.co.uk/news/business/news/accenture-one-of-worlds-biggest-companies-to-scrap-annual-performance-reviews-10421296.html.

Dalrymple, Theodore (2015) *Admirable Evasions: How Psychology Undermines Morality*. New York: Encounter Books.

Davies, Paul (1993) *The Mind of God: Science and the Search for Ultimate Meaning*. London: Penguin.

Dawkins, Richard (1996) A Survival Machine, *Edge*. Available at: https://www.edge.org/conversation/richard_dawkins-chapter-3-a-survival-machine.

Dennett, Daniel (1989) *The Intentional Stance*. Cambridge, MA: MIT Press.

Dennett, Daniel (1991) *Consciousness Explained*. Boston, MA: Little, Brown and Co.

Dennett, Daniel (1995) *Darwin's Dangerous Idea: Evolution and the Meanings of Life*. New York: Touchstone.

Deutsch, David (2011) *The Beginning of Infinity: Explanations That Transform the World*. London: Penguin.

Dostoevsky, Fyodor (2014 [1861]) *Notes from Underground*, tr. Kyril Zinovieff and Jenny Hughes. Richmond: Alma Classics.

Durkheim, Émile (1995 [1912]) *The Elementary Forms of Religious Life*, ed. and tr. Karen E. Fields. New York: Free Press.

Eagleton, Terry (2014) *Culture and the Death of God*. New Haven, CT: Yale University Press.

Eco, Umberto (2010 [2004]) *On Beauty: A History of a Western Idea*, tr. Alastair McEwen. London: MacLehose Press.

Edexcel (2017) *International GCSE Art and Design (9–1): Specification*. London: Edexcel.

Eliot, T. S. (2001 [1943]) *Four Quartets*. London: Faber & Faber.

Flood, Alison (2019) Study Finds *Mr Greedy* Rivals *Grapes of Wrath* in Reading Complexity, *The Guardian* (2 March). Available at: https://www.theguardian.com/books/2019/mar/02/study-finds-mr-greedy-rivals-grapes-of-wrath-in-reading-complexity.

Flynn, James (2009) *What Is Intelligence? Beyond the Flynn Effect*. Cambridge: Cambridge University Press.

Ford, Martin (2016) *The Rise of the Robots: Technology and the Threat of Mass Unemployment*. London: Oneworld Publications.

Forster, E. M. (1910) *Howards End*. Available at: http://www.online-literature.com/forster/howards_end/.

Fry, Stephen (2018) *Mythos: The Greek Myths Retold*. London: Penguin.

Gadamer, Hans-Georg (1989 [1975]) *Truth and Method*, tr. Joan Stambaugh. London: Bloomsbury.

Gibb, Nick (2017) Empowering Teachers to Deliver Greater Equity. Speech delivered at the International Summit on the Teaching Profession, Edinburgh, 30 March. Available at: https://www.gov.uk/government/speeches/nick-gibb-empowering-teachers-to-deliver-greater-equity.

Gopal, Priyamvada (2017) Yes, We Must Decolonise: Our Teaching Has to Go Beyond Elite White Men, *The Guardian* (27 October). Available at: https://www.theguardian.com/commentisfree/2017/oct/27/decolonise-elite-white-men-decolonising-cambridge-university-english-curriculum-literature.

Grange, Joseph (2004) *John Dewey, Confucius and Global Philosophy*. Albany, NY: State University of New York Press.

Griffin, Andrew (2016) Elon Musk: The Chance We Are Not Living in a Computer Simulation is 'One in Billions', *The Independent* (2 June). Available at: http://www.independent.co.uk/life-style/gadgets-and-tech/news/elon-musk-ai-artificial-intelligence-computer-simulation-gaming-virtual-reality-a7060941.html.

Haidt, Jonathan (2017) Wriston Lecture: The Age of Outrage: What It's Doing to Our Universities, and Our Country [video]. Speech delivered at the Manhattan Institute, New York, 15 November. Available at: https://www.manhattan-institute.org/html/2017-wriston-lecture-age-outrage-10779.html.

Harari, Yuval Noah (2017) *Homo Deus: A Brief History of Tomorrow*. New York: HarperCollins.

Harari, Yuval Noah (2018) *21 Lessons for the 21st Century*. London: Jonathan Cape.

Harris, Sam (2012) *Free Will*. New York: Free Press.

Harris, Sam (2017) What Is True? [interview with Jordan B. Peterson], *Making Sense with Sam Harris* [podcast] (21 January). Available at: https://www.youtube.com/watch?v=3OqrZs9sRHs.

Hart, Betty and Risley, Todd R. (1995) *Meaningful Differences in the Everyday Experience of Young American Children*. Baltimore, MD: Paul H. Brookes.

Hawking, Stephen (2012) Speech delivered at the Opening Ceremony of the London Paralympic Games, 29 August. Available at: http://www.ctc.cam.ac.uk/news/120829_newsitem.php.

Hegel, Georg Wilhelm Friedrich (2005 [1821]) *Elements of the Philosophy of Right* [Grundlinien der Philosophie des Rechts], tr. S. W. Dyde. New York: Dover.

Heidegger, Martin (2010 [1953]) *Being and Time*, tr. Joan Stambaugh. Albany, NY: State University of New York Press.

Hibbert, Christopher (1969) *The Grand Tour*. Weidenfeld & Nicolson.

Hirsch, Jr, Eric Donald (2006) *The Knowledge Deficit: Closing the Shocking Education Gap for American Children*. New York: Houghton Mifflin.

Husserl, Edmund (1970 [1936]) *The Crisis of European Sciences and Transcendental Phenomenology: An Introduction to Phenomenological Philosophy* (Die Krisis der europäischen Wissenschaften und die transzendentale Phänomenologie: Eine Einleitung in die phänomenologische Philosophie), tr. David Carr. Evanston, IL: Northwestern University Press.

Husserl, Edmund (2001 [1900–1901]) *Logical Investigations* (Logische Untersuchungen), 2 vols, tr. John N. Findlay. Abingdon and New York: Routledge.

James, C. L. R. (1980 [1966]) The Making of the Caribbean Peoples: Peasants and Workers, in *Spheres of Existence (Selected Writings)*. London: Allison & Busby.

James, C. L. R. (1980 [1969]) Discovering Literature in Trinidad: The Nineteen-Thirties, in *Spheres of Existence (Selected Writings)*. London: Allison & Busby.

Jasanoff, Alan (2018) The Cerebral Mystique, *Aeon* (8 May). Available at: https://aeon.co/essays/we-are-more-than-our-brains-on-neuroscience-and-being-human.

Jenkins, Simon (2018) *A Short History of Europe: From Pericles to Putin*. New York: Viking/Penguin Random House.

Keats, John (1899) 'Ode on a Grecian Urn' (1820). In *The Complete Poetical Works and Letters of John Keats* (Cambridge Edition). Boston, MA: Houghton Mifflin.

Keay, Lara (2017) Could Robots Replace Teachers Within 10 Years? University Vice Chancellor Claims Humans Will Only Be Classroom Assistants in the Future, *Daily Mail Online* (11 September). Available at: https://www.dailymail.co.uk/news/article-4871230/Robots-replace-teachers-10-years-says-academic.html.

Lewis, C. S. (2010 [1943]) *The Abolition of Man.* Las Vegas, NV: Lits.

Lewis, Paul (2017) 'Our Minds Can Be Hijacked': The Tech Insiders Who Fear a Smartphone Dystopia, *The Guardian* (6 October). Available at: https://www.theguardian.com/technology/2017/oct/05/smartphone-addiction-silicon-valley-dystopia.

Libet, Benjamin (1985) Unconscious Cerebral Initiative and the Role of Conscious Will in Voluntary Action, *Behavioral and Brain Sciences*, 8(4): 529–566.

Lilla, Mark (2016) The End of Identity Liberalism, *New York Times* (18 November). Available at: https://www.nytimes.com/2016/11/20/opinion/sunday/the-end-of-identity-liberalism.html.

London, Manuel (ed.) (2001) *How People Evaluate Others in Organizations.* New York: Lawrence Erlbaum Associates.

Ma, Jack (2018) Education is the Biggest Challenge [video]. Speech delivered at the University of Hong Kong, 18 May. Available at: https://www.youtube.com/watch?v=7fu40RRlMMk.

McGregor, Jena (2013) The Corporate Kabuki of Performance Reviews, *Washington Post* (14 February).

Marcus Aurelius (2002) *Meditations: A New Translation*, tr. Gregory Hays. New York: Modern Library.

Mason, Paul (2019) *Clear Bright Future: A Radical Defence of the Human Being.* London: Penguin Random House.

Melville, Herman (2003 [1851]) *Moby-Dick: or, The Whale.* New York: Penguin.

Midgley, Mary (1994) *The Ethical Primate: Humans, Freedom and Morality.* Abingdon and New York: Routledge.

Midgley, Mary (2004) *The Myths We Live By.* Abingdon and New York: Routledge.

Midgley, Mary (2005) *The Essential Mary Midgley*, ed. David Midgley. Abingdon and New York: Routledge.

Midgley, Mary (2014) *Are You An Illusion?* Abingdon and New York: Routledge.

Mill, John Stuart (2006 [1859]) *On Liberty* and *The Subjection of Women.* London: Penguin.

Millet, Lydia (2009) *How the Dead Dream.* London: Vintage.

Milne, A. A. (1956 [1928]) *The House at Pooh Corner.* New York: Puffin.

Mitchell, Kevin (2018a) How Free Is Our Will?, *Psychology Today* (25 November). Available at: https://www.psychologytoday.com/gb/blog/innate/201811/how-free-is-our-will.

Mitchell, Kevin (2018b) *Innate: How the Wiring of Our Brains Shapes Who We Are.* Princeton, NJ: Princeton University Press.

Mitchell, Kevin (2019) No Clones in the Classroom: Differences in Children's Psychology Can Be Amplified by Experience, *Psychology Today* (10 June). Available at: https://www.psychologytoday.com/gb/blog/innate/201906/no-clones-in-the-classroom.

Müller, Adam H. (1922) *Die Elemente der Staatskunst,* 2 vols, ed. Jakob Baxa. Jena: G. Fischer.

Nagel, Thomas (1979) Subjective and Objective, in *Mortal Questions.* Cambridge: Cambridge University Press, pp. 196–213.

Nietzsche, Friedrich (1969 [1883–1891]) *Thus Spoke Zarathustra,* tr. Reginald Hollingdale. London: Penguin.

Nietzsche, Friedrich (1998 [1887]) *On the Genealogy of Morality: A Polemic,* tr. Maudemarie Clark and Alan J. Swensen. Indianapolis, IN: Hackett Publishing.

Oakeshott, Michael (1962) The Voice of Poetry in the Conversation of Mankind, in *Rationalism in Politics and Other Essays.* New York: Basic Books, pp. 197–247.

Oakeshott, Michael (1989 [1975]) A Place of Learning, in Timothy Fuller (ed.), *The Voice of Liberal Learning: Michael Oakeshott.* Indianapolis, IN: Liberty Fund.

Ofsted (2018) *An Investigation Into How to Assess the Quality of Education Through Curriculum Intent, Implementation and Impact: Phase 3 Findings of Curriculum Research.* Ref: 180035. Available at: https://www.gov.uk/government/publications/curriculum-research-assessing-intent-implementation-and-impact.

Ofsted and Spielman, Amanda (2017) HMCI's Commentary: Recent Primary and Secondary Curriculum Research (11 October). Available at: https://www.gov.uk/government/speeches/hmcis-commentary-october-2017.

Olson, Gary (1990) Jacques Derrida on Rhetoric and Composition: A Conversation, *Journal of Advanced Composition,* 10(1): 1–21.

O'Neil, Cathy (2016) *Weapons of Math Destruction: How Big Data Increases Inequality and Threatens Democracy.* New York: Crown.

Orwell, George (2008 [1949]) *Nineteen Eighty-Four.* London: Penguin

Penrose, Roger (1994) *Shadows of the Mind: A Search for the Missing Science of Consciousness.* Oxford: Oxford University Press.

Pinker, Steven (2018) *Enlightenment Now: The Case for Reason, Science, Humanism, and Progress.* New York: Penguin.

Plomin, Robert (2018) *Blueprint: How DNA Makes Us Who We Are.* London: Penguin.

Polanyi, Michael (1966) *The Tacit Dimension.* Chicago, IL: University of Chicago Press.

Postman, Neil (1996) The End of Education [video]. Available at: https://www.youtube.com/watch?v=3G8a4Tdnab8.

Pound, Ezra (1977 [1948]) *Ezra Pound and Music: The Complete Criticism.* New York: New Directions.

Rand, Ayn (1971) *The Romantic Manifesto: A Philosophy of Literature.* New York: New American Library.

Reisz, Matthew (2015) Is Philosophy Dead? *Times Higher Education* (22 February). Available at: https://www.timeshighereducation.com/news/is-philosophy-dead/2018686.article.

Robinson, Martin (2013) *Trivium 21c: Preparing Young People for the Future with Lessons from the Past.* Carmarthen: Independent Thinking Press.

Robson, David (2019) *The Intelligence Trap: Why Smart People Do Stupid Things and How to Make Wiser Decisions.* London: Hodder & Stoughton.

Rousseau, Jean-Jacques (1923 [1762]) *The Social Contract* [Du contrat social], tr. G. D. H. Cole. London and Toronto: J.M. Dent and Sons.

Rovelli, Carlo (2016) *Seven Brief Lessons on Physics.* New York: Riverhead Books.

Rovelli, Carlo (2018) *The Order of Time.* New York: Allen Lane.

Scott, Belita and Vidakovic, Ivana (2018) Teacher Well-Being and Workload Survey, *Ofsted Blog* (30 November). Available at: https://educationinspection.blog.gov.uk/2018/11/30/teacher-well-being-and-workload-survey-interim-findings/.

Scruton, Roger (2000) *Modern Culture.* London: Continuum.

Scruton, Roger (2010) *The Uses of Pessimism and the Danger of False Hope.* Oxford: Oxford University Press.

Scruton, Roger (2016) *The Soul of the World.* Princeton, NJ: Princeton University Press.

Scruton, Roger (2017) *Where We Are: The State of Britain Now.* London: Bloomsbury.

Shaw, Julia (2016) *The Memory Illusion: Remembering, Forgetting and the Science of False Memory.* London: Penguin Random House.

Sheldrake, Rupert (2012) *The Science Delusion.* London: Coronet.

Siedentop, Larry (2015) *Inventing the Individual: The Origins of Western Liberalism.* London: Penguin.

Sky News (2017) Education Revolution: 'AI Machines Will Replace Teachers', Claims Academic (11 September). Available at: https://news.sky.com/story/ai-machines-will-replace-teachers-claims-wellington-college-head-11029135.

Snow, Charles Percy (1998 [1964]) *The Two Cultures.* Cambridge: Cambridge University Press.

Social Mobility Commission (2016) *State of the Nation 2016: Social Mobility in Great Britain* (November). Available at: https://www.gov.uk/government/news/state-of-the-nation-report-on-social-mobility-in-great-britain.

Stenhouse, Lawrence (1975) *An Introduction to Curriculum Research and Development.* London: Heinemann.

Sulleyman, Aatif (2017) The Singularity: AI Will Make Humans Sexier and Funnier, Says Google Expert, *The Independent* (16 March). Available at: http://www.independent.co.uk/life-style/gadgets-and-tech/news/singularity-artificial-intelligence-humans-sexy-funny-ai-music-art-google-futurist-engineering-ray-a7633481.html.

Tallis, Raymond (2005) *The Knowing Animal: A Philosophical Enquiry Into Knowledge and Truth.* Edinburgh: Edinburgh University Press.

Turing, Alan M. (1950) Computing Machinery and Intelligence, *Mind*, 59 (October): 433–460.

Valente, Patricia M. (2016) How Do the Arts Nurture and Connect Emotions, in Linda L. Lyman (ed.), *Brain Science for Principals: What School Leaders Need to Know*. Lanham, MD: Rowman & Littlefield, pp. 85–90.

Walker, Alice (2000) *The Way Forward Is With a Broken Heart*. New York: Ballantine.

Watson, Peter (2005) *Ideas: A History of Thought and Invention, from Fire to Freud*. New York: HarperCollins.

Weber, Max (1992 [1904–1905]) *The Protestant Ethic and the Spirit of Capitalism*, tr. T. Parsons. Abingdon and New York: Routledge.

Whitman, Walt (1959) *Leaves of Grass*. New York: Penguin.

Williams, Bernard (2002) *Truth and Truthfulness: An Essay in Genealogy*. Princeton, NJ: Princeton University Press.

Wood, Stewart (2014) Juncture Interview: Roberto Unger on the Means and Ends of the Political Left, *IPPR* (22 January). Available at: https://www.ippr.org/juncture/juncture-interview-roberto-unger-on-the-means-and-ends-of-the-political-left.

Young, Michael (2001) Down with Meritocracy, *The Guardian* (29 June). Available at: https://www.theguardian.com/politics/2001/jun/29/comment.

Young, Michael (2014) The Curriculum and the Entitlement to Knowledge. Edited text of a talk given at a seminar organised by Cambridge Assessment Network, 25 March, Magdalene College, Cambridge. Available at: http://www.cambridgeassessment.org.uk/Images/166279-the-curriculum-and-the-entitlement-to-knowledge-prof-michael-young.pdf.

Yousafzai, Malala (2013) *I Am Malala: The Girl Who Stood Up for Education and Was Shot by the Taliban*. London: Weidenfeld & Nicolson.

Zakaria, Fareed (2015) *In Defense of a Liberal Education*. New York: W.W. Norton.

Zeman, Adam (2004) *Consciousness: A User's Guide*. New Haven, CT: Yale University Press.

Zeman, Adam (2009) *A Portrait of the Brain*. New Haven, CT: Yale University Press.

Index

Trivium in Practice

Martin Robinson

ISBN: 978-178135243-4

Trivium in Practice brings together a series of case studies written by educators who were inspired by Martin Robinson's first book, *Trivium 21c*. Taken together, these case studies reveal how, regardless of setting or sector, the trivium can deliver a truly great education for our children.

Great teaching has the three elements of the trivium at its centre. Grammar: foundational knowledge and skills. Dialectic: questioning, thinking and practising. Rhetoric: the ability to express oneself beautifully, persuasively and articulately in any form.

The trivium is a helpful way for a teacher to think about the art of teaching. Through the model of the trivium traditional values and progressive ideals can coexist; both knowledge and cultural capital matter and skills are interwoven with content. The trivium isn't a gimmick to be imposed on to a curriculum; it is a tried and tested approach to education. It is the key to great teaching and learning, as this group of educators discovered.

Trivium 21c

Preparing young people for the future with lessons from the past

Martin Robinson

ISBN: 978-178135054-6

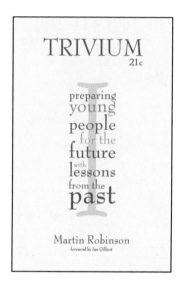

From Ancient Greece to the present day, *Trivium 21c* explores whether a contemporary trivium (Grammar, Dialectic, and Rhetoric) can unite progressive and traditionalist institutions, teachers, politicians and parents in the common pursuit of providing a great education for our children in the 21st century.

Education policy and practice is a battleground. Traditionalists argue for the teaching of a privileged type of hard knowledge and deride soft skills. Progressives deride learning about great works of the past, preferring '21c skills' (21st century skills) such as creativity and critical thinking.

Whilst looking for a school for his daughter, the author became frustrated by schools' inability to value knowledge, as well as creativity, foster discipline alongside free-thinking, and value citizenship alongside independent learning. Drawing from his work as a creative teacher, Robinson finds inspiration in the arts and the need to nurture learners with the ability to deal with the uncertainties of our age.